The Travels of
Sherlock Holmes

Also by John Hall

I Remember the Date Very Well
One Hundred and Forty Different Varieties
Unexplored Possibilities
The Dynamics of a Falling Star
Guilty of Several Monographs
Some Knowledge of Baritsu (with Hirayama Yuichi)
Sidelights on Holmes

The Travels of Sherlock Holmes

John Hall

**BREESE
BOOKS
LONDON**

First published in 1997 by
Breese Books Ltd
164 Kensington Park Road, London W11 2ER, England

© Breese Books Ltd, 1997

ISBN: 0 947533 27 3

Front cover photograph
is reproduced by kind permission of
Retrograph Archive, London

Typeset in 11½/14pt Caslon by
Ann Buchan (Typesetters), Middlesex
Printed and bound in Great Britain by
Itchen Printers Ltd, Southampton

For Joy,
with love

PART ONE

From the journals of Dr John H Watson

1

Encounters in an east wind

It is only to be expected that there have been many requests that I should give some account of the valuable, indeed invaluable, work which Mr Sherlock Holmes rendered his country in the recent dreadful war. It is true that there are a good many tales of those terrible years which I might share with my readers. But many of the episodes in which we were involved are so fantastic, and so very many of the memories are still so acutely painful to me, that it may well be some considerable time before I can accede fully to these requests.

By way of some slight compensation, I shall instead now lay before the public, ever eager for tidings of Holmes, however out-of-date those tidings may be, a story as fantastic as any of those which I must temporarily suppress, a story which has remained untold for some three decades. I myself was in ignorance of the true facts for two of those decades, and thereafter Holmes's own prohibition prevented me from furnishing the public with any sort of account. Only now have circumstances which I shall not dwell upon made it possible for me to tell this story.

I am conscious that I cannot tell my tale as it should be told. I personally did not take any part in it, but heard it only gradually, at second or third hand, as you will see as we proceed. For that reason, I have adopted the same narrative style as in the very first story in which I had the privilege of introducing Mr Sherlock Holmes to his many admirers. That is to say, I have included those sections in which I myself had no part – and that is necessarily the greater portion of this tale – in almost the exact form in which I heard them or read them, with only such editing as is necessary for the sake of clarity.

However, this time I have not dignified my own small contributions by referring to them as part of my 'reminiscences.' That phrase was a literary conceit foisted upon me by editors, publishers and an over-enthusiastic literary agent. I have often regretted allowing myself to be persuaded as to the advisability of its use, for it has returned to haunt me, causing me many an embarrassing moment when complete strangers have accosted me on railway platforms, demanding to know where they could buy a copy of the *Reminiscences*, and expressing rank disbelief when I informed them that there is as yet no such work extant.

So far as I am concerned, then, the story began in those dark days in the midst of the Great War, the 'War to end wars.' That east wind of which Holmes had spoken in that fateful August of 1914 had blown, and blown with a vengeance. And many of us had, as he had foretold, withered before its blast.

At the very start of the war, it had been my intention to volunteer for active service. One might be forgiven for thinking that so modest and laudable an ambition would be achieved without difficulty. However, I was soon to be made aware that it would not.

For over two weeks, I was shuffled from one impossibly young man to the next, asked to divulge every personal detail as to myself, my career, and my life in general, and given countless smudged forms to fill in, each identical to its predecessor, and each requiring me to answer an inordinate number of irrelevant and impertinent questions.

I am usually a tolerant man – indeed, I take a slight pride in my Bohemianism of disposition. Still, there is a proverb about worms and turnings, and one afternoon, in an obscure office somewhere in Whitehall, as I was asked politely enough to sit down yet again and answer a few more questions, my patience came to an end.

I recall that I had taken a bottle of Beaune with my lunch – it was, even in those early days of the conflict, becoming somewhat difficult to find – and perhaps that had some effect, I cannot say.

I can say that, so far from sitting down quietly, I thumped the desk angrily. 'No, sir,' said I, 'I will not sit down! Will you kindly tell me just one thing? How may I be of some small service to my country, Dr – Dr –' and here I bethought me to glance at the name plate on the desk before me – 'Dr Stamford?'

The young man cleared his throat in a nervous way, but before he could speak, a thought struck me, and I went on, in more measured tones, 'I knew a Dr Stamford, many years ago. He was a dresser under me, at old Bart's.'

The young man shot me a keen glance. 'Why,' said he, 'that would have been my father!' He riffled through the papers in front of him, consulted one of them, then said, 'Dr John Watson? The writer? The *Strand* Dr Watson? The friend and colleague of Mr Sherlock Holmes? Sir, my father has spoken of you more times than I could say. Indeed, he's dined out upon his acquaintance with you this past twenty years.'

It was then that I did sit down, shaken to my core, not by thus being recognized – something which I have perforce grown used to since I met Holmes – but by the full import of what he had just told me.

'Young Stamford – I mean, your father, of course – he is

well?' was all that I could manage to stammer out.

'He is, thank you, Dr Watson.'

'I beg your pardon, Dr Stamford,' I said in a more civil tone than I had been using up until then. 'I fear I have been wasting a good deal of time. Both my own, which is not worth very much, and yours, which is. I see that, although wars are started by foolish old men, they must be fought by clever young ones. Would to God that it were the other way round!'

'You see, sir,' said he earnestly, with an evident desire to be helpful, 'the trouble lies in your insistence on this phrase "active service". If I may speak plainly?'

'Please do.'

'For the moment, at any rate, we are looking for men much younger than yourself for what we might term the rough and tumble work. Naturally enough, we rather hesitate to say as much outright to so distinguished a colleague as yourself, particularly when you have been one of the first to volunteer.'

'I quite understand. I shall not embarrass you further. My compliments to your father, when next you see him.' I rose to go, a good deal more shaken than I would have cared to admit.

Stamford waved me back to my chair. 'If I might venture on a suggestion which may appeal to your patriotic desire to be of use?'

'By all means.'

'The general mobilization does mean that there are a good many recruits who must undergo a preliminary medical examination before they are assigned to their regiments. And as most of the young – ah, that is, less experienced – medical men are required, or will be required, elsewhere, it would be most helpful if an extremely experienced doctor such as yourself might be called upon –'

'Please do not say any more,' I told him. 'Just tell me when and where I am needed.'

Young Stamford – young, indeed! – rose, and held out his hand, the relief patent in his face. 'It is extremely good of you, Dr Watson,' said he.

A couple of days later, I received my instructions, and soon after there commenced one of the most painful episodes of my career.

I have seen dreadful wounds at the battle of Maiwand in Afghanistan. I have viewed some of the victims of that maniac of the East End who styled himself the 'Ripper', in the company of Holmes, whose advice on the case might have cleared up the matter at once, had it been heeded by the arrogant Sir Charles Warren. So it will be understood that I am not exactly squeamish.

I may perhaps be believed, then, when I assert that the only comparison that comes to mind, when thinking of the pitiful selection of humanity which paraded before me and the other members of the various medical boards at that time, is the sorry array on the marble slabs in the dissecting room.

Concave of chest and flat of foot, deformed with rickets, and worse, the men whom we expected to fight for us – and die for us – would scarcely have been fitted to do anything more taxing than run a whelk stall at some very unfrequented seaside resort. Summoned from slums little different from the rookeries of Dickens in order to fight for a country that had at last remembered their existence, they blinked at the daylight with watery, myopic eyes, like something discovered on turning over a flat stone.

It was a disgrace to a land which has been called 'Mother of the Free', and the sole consolation is that the warmongers who had begun the whole thing were so shaken that they determined that something must be done – although,

God knows, they were in no particular hurry once the war was over and done with, nor are they now.

But I fear I digress. A week of this work fairly broke my spirit, and I contacted young Stamford once more. I suspect that he was by now thoroughly sick of the sight of me, but he hid it well enough, and once I had explained to him how matters stood, he promised to move me to more congenial work.

He was as good as his word. A fortnight after my interview with him, I was moved to a convalescent hospital in Surrey. It had originally been a manor house, but the owner had died, or gone off to the front, or turned it over to the War Office in public-spirited fashion, I never knew exactly. It was set in a large and well-maintained park, and at no great distance from a pretty little village.

The surroundings were delightful, then, and the other members of the medical staff, men of around my own age, were for the most part excellent companions. The nurses, too, mainly attractive young women from good families, lent a good deal of charm to the place, although naturally enough they mostly had eyes for the patients rather than the superannuated doctors such as myself.

These patients were mostly surgical cases sent to us not for any immediate or urgent treatment, which they had already received, but for rest and quiet before being returned to action, or – with dreadful frequency – being discharged, useless for further duty, into civilian life, of whatever sort it might chance to be for the unfortunate fellows. We saw one or two cases of 'neurasthenia' or 'shell shock', as the current argot had it, poor devils whose minds had been pushed beyond human endurance, though most of these cases went for special treatment elsewhere.

Sometimes we had more acute cases on our hands. Although the majority of our patients had undergone surgery before ever they reached the place, and been passed as ready for the convalescence for which they came to us, yet there were nevertheless relatively minor infections, which should not and would not have bothered a healthy constitution, but which met with little resistance from weakened men. And there were occasional cases of a wound, too hastily treated in the heat of battle, turning septic, so that we had our occasional losses, though, thank God, these were few and far between.

One such sad case was a Major Harold Dyce, who had sustained some dreadful injuries in some unsung act of bravery. By rights, he should hardly have come to us in his weakened state, but we did our best, and were reasonably optimistic that he might make a full recovery, when, as ill-luck would have it, one of those secondary infections which I have mentioned set in, and thereafter his decline was a rapid one.

The custom of the place was for one of the doctors to be on call at night, in case of emergency, and on one of my own duty nights, the sister in charge called me to Dyce's room – he was ill enough to have been put on his own – saying she thought he had not long to live.

I saw at once that she was right, and since there were no other patients who seemed likely to need my attention that night, I told the sister that I would stay and give Dyce what comfort I might, and she accordingly returned to her own station.

There was, indeed, little that needed to be done. Dyce was sleeping, a sleep that would, I was certain, merge imperceptibly into that greater sleep that awaits us all, and I decided to doze while I might, for I could be reached there as well as anywhere, if anything more pressing intervened.

Towards three in the morning, when the line between

life and death is at its thinnest, I woke to find Dyce also awake, and trying to speak.

Thinking that he might have some last words for his family, I bent over him trying to hear what he said.

'Who's that?' said he, seeing me bend over him.

'It's Dr Watson. Try to rest.'

'Watson?' He smiled, with an obvious effort. 'Good old Watson!'

'That's right,' said I. 'Good old Watson. Try –'

'He used to say that.'

'Who?' I asked, humouring him in the best medical tradition, but suspecting it was nothing more than the final stages of delirium.

'Why, Mr Sherlock Holmes, of course.'

I was astounded, for I had never heard him speak of Holmes before. 'Holmes?' said I, forgetting for the moment that he was my patient. 'Do you know Holmes, then?'

'I did, in Tibet, and Persia,' said Dyce.

'Why, in that case, I am indeed "Good old Watson,"' said I, 'for I have been Holmes's friend for many years, and in fact I wrote accounts of many of his cases.'

'For the *Strand*?' said Dyce, his breath coming in great gulps now.

'Yes,' said I, fearful now that even this slight exertion had overtaxed his feeble strength. 'Now, you must try to rest, and we'll talk about it all later.'

By way of an answer, he waved to the little table by his side, where his few meagre possessions were stacked. 'Case,' said he, speaking with great difficulty.

I picked up an old leather attaché case from the table. 'This?'

'Open – open it.'

I did so, and took out a squat octavo notebook bound in faded green leather.

'Want – you – to have it.'

'But your family –' I began.

'No – family. Want – you –' and he never said more in this world.

I did what was necessary – God knows, there were funerals enough in those days for us all to have become proficient in their arrangement – and then I made some enquiries into Dyce's background before I thought of embarking on an examination of the book he had summarily bequeathed to me. I found that, as he had said, there was no record of any next of kin, and further investigation showed that the bulk of the friends he had made in his regiment had perished in the early days of the fighting.

By the time I had established all this, I had half forgotten about the book, which I had placed at the back of a drawer. And, for some time, my own work, which had increased somewhat as the war progressed, prevented me from looking at the book. So it was not until some considerable time after Dyce's death that I actually found time to sit down and begin to take a preliminary glance through it.

That preliminary glance, which was all I had originally intended to give the book, was sufficient to rivet my attention. I sat far longer than I had planned, into the small hours of the morning, reading almost half the book without a pause. The first few pages were disjointed notes, the journal of a man on active service as it seemed, but then followed a second, much longer section, which was evidently an attempt to make a cohesive narrative from the earlier notes. I read on and on, unable to break off from my task, until dawn found me with a thick head, and a sense partly of anger, and wholly of astonishment.

At that time I was, as one might imagine, seeing very little of Holmes. My own work kept me at the hospital, while Holmes was away, Heaven alone knew where, on one or more of those mysterious errands which I had grown to know so well in the course of my friendship with him. The times being as they were, it was scarcely to be expected that he would write with news of his whereabouts or his doings. I did attempt to contact his brother, by this time Sir Mycroft Holmes, GCB, GCMG, KCSI, etc., but was unable to reach that great and exceedingly busy man, who was, I felt sure, overseeing the waging of the war pretty much on his own.

A year or so went by, during the course of which I was obliged to put the matter of Dyce's journal, with its queer tale, to the back of my mind. And, once there, it faded gradually from my thoughts, as matters which are not of immediate moment have a habit of doing. Still, I frequently recalled it to mind, when thoughts of the old days returned unbidden, or someone said something to remind me of my time in Baker Street, and more than once I retrieved the journal, and read through it with the same amazement as I had felt on that first occasion.

Time rolled inexorably on. I was due some leave, and as things were fairly quiet at the hospital just then, the war having settled down into a kind of stalemate in the mud of Flanders, I had no compunction about taking it.

I went up to London, putting up at a private hotel in the Strand, just as I had done thirty years or more before, though now I was somewhat less concerned about the weekly charges than I had been in those early days.

I found London to be a peculiar place. The most obvious change from pre-war days was the almost total absence of young men, which gave the capital a strange, lop-sided look. And very many of the women were in some sort of uniform, or busy with work other than shopping. On my first day, I boarded a bus, and was surprised to find that my fare was collected by a very attractive young woman. Surprise turned to astonishment when, as I left the bus, I noticed that the driver was also a woman!

It was, to be sure, an interesting experience to see London under these conditions, unique in all my long and varied acquaintance with the capital, but the fascination of the place soon began to wear thin, and, after a very few days of wandering about alone, I had all but decided to cut my leave short and get back to work.

Before sending a telegram to the hospital to let them know to expect me back early, I went into the Long Bar of the old Cri for one last drink. As my readers will be aware, the place had some sentimental associations for me, for it was there that my acquaintance with Sherlock Holmes might be said to have begun. Even so, at first it had all the earmarks of yet another depressing *recherché du temps perdu*, such as my entire visit had thus far proved to be.

It was the lunch hour, and the place should have been crowded, yet it was deserted by comparison with the old days. There were, indeed, little knots of men here and there along the length of the bar, old dugouts such as myself, and younger officers who had managed to wangle some leave. They tried their best to be normal, cheerful, but their conversation was appalling to hear, a sort of forced gaiety, a hollow pretence that all was exactly as it had been.

I took the brandy and soda which the aged barman reluctantly handed to me, and moved to the far end of the bar, which was quiet and almost deserted. I had just raised the glass to my lips, when a familiar voice at my shoulder remarked, 'Drinking alone, Watson? A most dangerous course of action, as you, a doctor, should be aware.'

'Holmes!' I cried, almost – but not quite – spilling my drink in my agitation.

Holmes – for it was indeed my old friend, looking not much different from the Holmes of former days – laughed in the peculiar noiseless way he had, and suggested that we sit down, 'For,' said he, 'we have much to talk over.'

We found a table in a dark corner, and I sat down. 'Holmes,' I began severely, 'I have a bone to pick with you.'

'That sounds serious, Doctor.'

'It is. You have lied to me, Holmes.'

He raised an eyebrow. 'Indeed? And how, pray?'

'The entire tale of your absence from London after the death – the supposed death, that is – of Professor Moriarty was pure invention.'

'Indeed?' he repeated calmly. 'And how do you know that?'

'I have recently read the journal of one Harold Dyce.'

Holmes's brow furrowed in thought. 'Lieutenant Dyce?'

'Major,' I said. 'Or rather, he was. He gave me the journal by way of a legacy.'

'Ah,' said Holmes. 'He was a good man, Watson. Did you have much talk with him?'

'There was no time, I fear.'

'You would have liked him; he resembled you in many respects. So, he's dead, too? It's a sad business, Watson. The best of us are going. What sort of a world will the poor relicts who survive find to live in, I wonder?'

'Be all that as it may,' said I, 'Dyce's journal shows a very different tale from the one you told me, the one which I – in all good faith, Holmes – passed on to my readers. To speak plainly, I am a little bitter, and more than a little hurt, that you should choose not merely to refrain from confiding in me, but indeed tell me a downright fabrication.'

'Watson, Watson,' said he. 'Always Mr Valiant-for-truth! I assure you, Doctor, that it was quite essential that the full facts be kept from the general public, and your own forthright character would have prevented your acceding fully to the necessary deception. You have read the journal, you say?'

'I have.'

'Then you will already have begun to grasp something of the full story of those three years, and to realize that it was – then, at least – quite impossible that the true facts should be divulged. The implications for international relations would have been catastrophic.' He sighed loudly. 'Now, of course, anything which I can tell you could scarcely make things worse than they are, so I suppose I had better be honest, although it might be as well if you were to keep this to yourself, for the time being at any rate.' He stood up. 'Come along.'

'Where are we going?'

Holmes laughed heartily. 'Where do you think?'

'Not Baker Street?'

'Where else?'

'But – surely – you were retired, Holmes, to Surrey or some such rural backwater, as I understood it.'

Holmes smiled at my bewilderment. 'Close enough, and the old rooms were let to a young man.' The smile faded. 'However, he, like many of his brothers, has no further use for the rooms, so I was able to acquire a familiar *pied-à-terre* for as long as the present unpleasantness might last. Come.'

2

Mr Sherlock Holmes explains

W e set off towards Baker Street, walking briskly, for it was a chilly autumn day. I remarked upon the fact that Holmes, who set a good pace, seemed as fit as ever.

He turned those wonderfully penetrating eyes upon me, and said, 'I am, praise be, Watson. But if you should think of publishing any further accounts of my work – my work before the onset of the present business, I mean to say – before the present business is quite finished, you would oblige me by suggesting that I am now wholly retired. Possibly you might even mention that my health leaves much to be desired.'

'If you wish it, Holmes. But why?' I asked, puzzled.

'Because, Doctor, my enemies at the moment are even better organized, possess more resources, and are, if possible, even more unforgiving than Professor Moriarty or Colonel Moran ever were.'

'Indeed? And just who –'

'It would therefore be of the greatest service to me, and I may venture to say, to the country we both love, if they believed me to be quite out of things these days. So, if you should happen to be cajoled into contributing one of your sensational accounts to the popular press – something as to the arrest of Von Bork, perhaps, would catch the popular mood at present – then please do not be afraid to exaggerate the effects of time. Suggest that rheumatism prevents my getting about too briskly these days, or something of the kind.'

We halted before the old familiar door, and Holmes, after rummaging for some time through his pockets, gave a little grunt of annoyance. 'I appear to have lost my key,' he said. 'Would you oblige me by touching the bell, Watson?'

I felt acutely embarrassed for him, particularly after his recent remarks as to his being impervious to the passage of time, for the Holmes I had known of old would never have done anything so inconsequential as forget a key. But it would have been most impolite to draw attention to it, so I said nothing, merely contenting myself with ringing the bell.

The door was opened by a middle-aged woman of the landlady class, attractive enough in an overblown fashion. 'Yes, sir? Oh, it's you, Mr Holmes. Forget your key, did you?'

I glanced at Holmes, who stood a little way behind me, and was astounded to see that he was absolutely convulsed with that silent mirth of his. But he merely produced a key from his coat pocket, and held it aloft. 'I thought that I had done so, Mrs Wiggins, but I find I have it here after all.'

'Mrs Wiggins?' said I, looking from one to another of them. 'Nothing to do with young Wiggins, the little captain of irregulars, surely?'

'Why sir,' said Mrs Wiggins, beaming, 'I'm his wife.'

'Good Lord!'

'Yes, Doctor,' said Holmes, laughing aloud now at my astonishment, 'the inexorable passage of time affects us all alike.'

'Nor he ain't all that young, these days, nor yet that little,' added Mrs Wiggins. 'Begging your pardon, sir.'

'No, no, I suppose he isn't. But I last saw him when he

was fourteen or so, and went off to look for honest work, do you know, and so I suppose I remember him as he was. Is he in, or – no, he would surely be just too old for any sort of duty?' said I.

Mrs Wiggins cast what looked like an apprehensive glance at Holmes.

'He was well enough when I left him,' said Holmes, in a low tone.

'You mean –'

'Later, Doctor, later.' Holmes led the way inside, and I followed, up the seventeen most famous steps in all London, and into the old rooms.

I stood in the doorway, and gazed affectionately round. The row of scrapbooks stood on its accustomed shelf, the mantelpiece was invisible under its litter of pipes and envelopes – though I was pleased to observe that there was now no sign of a hypodermic syringe amongst the detritus.

Indeed, very little, if anything, seemed to have changed, save that the dust seemed to have ossified in places around some of the relics of Holmes's cases, which looked for all the world like an assortment of fossils displayed in a section through the carboniferous limestone.

'Did the previous tenant take the rooms furnished, then?' I asked innocently.

'Oh, Mycroft volunteered to look after many of my souvenirs temporarily, and he is even more careless in the matter of housekeeping than I am,' said Holmes in an offhand fashion, handing me a more generous measure of whisky than any I had seen since the outbreak of war, and waving me to a chair.

'Imagine young Wiggins married,' I said. 'And a father, no doubt?'

'Eight fine children,' said Holmes.

'Good God.'

'Wiggins is currently acting under my directions,' Holmes went on, 'and rendering the government sterling service. But we will return to that later, with your permission.'

'Very well. And now, Holmes, I have had something approaching an apology for having been misled, and an assurance that it was strictly necessary for the good of the international situation, both of which I am in a mood to accept,' I said. 'But what I have not had is a true account of what really took place.'

'No, and it is long overdue. First of all, Watson, you must surely have had some doubts concerning the events surrounding my disappearance and supposed death in 1891, to say nothing of my near-miraculous reappearance three years later? There were too many loose ends to satisfy a writer of your calibre, I imagine?'

'At the time, events were moving so rapidly that one had no time to think about things,' I told him. 'And then later, what with believing you to be dead, and then my wife – you understand –'

'Quite so,' said Holmes, in a soothing tone. 'But later?'

'Oh, later, there were a good many questions left unanswered. But so long as I was actively associated with you in your work, then the case we had in hand at the time was usually so exciting that I quite forgot about the earlier ones.'

'Yes, they were stirring times, were they not?'

'However, some of my readers did not forget, and I used to get all sorts of letters from people with time on their hands and nothing better to do with it, asking why I had put such-and-such a case in a year that was manifestly impossible, and the like. Still do get them. Damned impertinent nonsense! For some reason, clergymen seem particularly prone to that sort of quibbling,' I added reminiscently.

'What was your reply?' asked Holmes, his eyes twinkling.

'Well, doctors are notorious for their bad handwriting, so that, together with laying much of the blame at the printer's door, usually serves.'

'I see. A fascinating insight into the tricks of the writer's trade. But I imagine that you yourself were not quite so easily satisfied?'

'I may have had occasional doubts,' I said. 'And yet I knew that I had lived through those stirring times, as you call them, and that my accounts were, broadly speaking, correct. If any minor details were not quite right, I assumed that it was due to my being so busy at the time that I had misread the situation, or to a trifling lapse of memory since the events took place.'

'I have often thought,' said Holmes, 'that you are the ideal colleague for a man in my profession.'

'Indeed?' said I, my artless pride at the compliment mixed with mild astonishment, for Holmes was seldom bountiful with his praise.

'Indeed. You are so single-minded in your pursuit of the obvious that anything even slightly off the main track comes as a glorious surprise to you.'

'Ah.' He had not, I realized, changed in the slightest.

'You will, I am sure,' he went on, 'not easily have forgotten the late Professor Moriarty?'

'The famous scientific criminal, the – what was it you once called him – the Napoleon of crime?'

Holmes nodded, and laughed in his peculiar silent fashion.

'Indeed I have not forgotten him, Holmes,' I went on. 'The only foeman worthy of our steel? The – I quote from memory again, here – the organizer of half that was evil and almost all that went undetected in London? Or he was, until – until what, exactly, Holmes? For Dyce's journal tells a very different tale from what you had led me to believe.'

Sherlock Holmes put the tips of his fingers together, and stared at the ceiling with a dreamy expression in his eyes. 'The first thing to bear in mind,' said he, 'is that my investigations had hit Moriarty hard. There can be no doubt whatever upon that score. He was rattled when he came to see me in the April of 1891, rattled a good deal more than he dared admit, even to himself. Why should he, who had built up an enormous criminal empire in secret – an empire whose very existence depended upon total concealment – show his hand so openly in that way, had that empire not been shaken to its very foundations? I am convinced – for remember that we had never met before that day, though I had observed him from a distance – I am convinced that he thought me nothing more than a run-of-the-mill private detective, a man who could be bullied or bought with not the slightest difficulty.'

'But your reputation, Holmes?'

'Based on newspaper reports? Remember that at the time, you yourself had published only two accounts of my work, and –' he hesitated.

'And neither had done particularly well?' I asked.

'Well, let us say rather that the public did not appreciate a good thing quite as soon as they might have,' said Holmes. 'But the fact remains, the bulk of the references to my work had appeared in the popular press, which is very often far from trustworthy.'

'And Moriarty, having realized his mistake when he tried to threaten you, then resorted to trying to kill you?'

Holmes nodded. 'He had evidently not taken the possibility that I would resist his threats or blandishments into account, for he had made no proper plans to have me eliminated. That is clearly shown by the three very amateurish attempts on my life, a runaway van, a brick dropped from a rooftop, and what have you. If Moriarty had believed that his threats would be unsuccessful, he would have had Moran waiting outside this house in a cab, his air-gun at the ready.'

'And yet you were shaken by those three attempts, amateur though they may have been, when you visited me the same day,' said I. 'I'll swear to that.'

'I was, Watson. You see, threats having failed, the only possible course left open to Moriarty was to ensure that I did not appear as a witness against him. The evidence was so complex that, without me there, a clever barrister could gain an acquittal without much difficulty.'

'As happened with Moran?'

'Exactly as happened with Moran. And some other high-placed members of the gang, Moriarty's most trusted lieutenants. Had I been at the trial, there is not the slightest doubt that Moran and those others would have hanged. I knew that, and Moriarty knew that. The first bungled attempts on my life having failed, I was frightened lest Moriarty, grown desperate, should make more elaborate plans that might succeed. Not that I was frightened for myself, or at any rate not more than any sensible man would have been, but I saw the entire case, years of work, being destroyed, utterly wasted by my death. My needless death at that, for by going abroad for a week or so – and I had originally intended no longer a stay than that – I could remain out of danger until the police had done their part.'

'Hence the apparently motiveless journey?'

'Just so.'

'One thing puzzles me,' I said. 'When we had evaded Moriarty at Chelmsford, or wherever it may have been, you said you thought he would get on to Paris, and watch our luggage, which we had abandoned on the train. Did you then expect him to return to London, to face arrest?'

Holmes raised an eyebrow.

I went on, 'I ask not because I ever thought anything of it myself, but because I had a most unpleasant half hour with a very large, very irascible old man in Simpson's, ten years or so ago now. Was he really expected to believe that Moriarty, the criminal genius of the age, a crook with the intellectual capacity of Sherlock Holmes, would behave in so idiotic a fashion, and so on and so forth? I couldn't eat my chop in peace. Fellow kept poking me in the chest, demanding an answer.'

Holmes flung back his head and laughed. 'And you had no answer to give him? Poor Watson. No, when I said Moriarty would "get on to Paris," I meant to say nothing more than that he would contact his agents in France, and they would do the watching. I knew he was in the process of extending his operations to the Continent, if he had not already done so.'

'Indeed?'

'Indubitably. The dates he had quoted to me, as recorded by you in the account which you somewhat theatrically entitled "The Final Problem", demonstrated that fact quite conclusively. No, Moriarty himself dared not leave England, for he was busy trying to save what he could from the coming storm. He had a contact — and perhaps more than one — in the official police. I had long suspected that, and tested my theory when he spoke to me, by the very simple expedient of mentioning that the police would act on the following Monday. He never turned a hair, and later in our talk he spoke of it in terms which clearly showed that he already knew before ever he called upon me.'

'There was a danger in it, though?' I said. 'Had he not known —'

Holmes waved a hand impatiently. 'I was quite convinced

that he did know. And I was right. Because he knew so many of the details, he thought he might be able to save the entire organization – his plans, remember, were always on the grand scale – but for once he had overestimated his own abilities. When the crash came, when it was finally and inescapably clear that he would be taken if he remained, then he fled precipitately.'

'Another point bothers me,' I said. 'I can understand Moriarty's wanting to kill you, after what you had done to him, but I cannot really see why he was so careless of his own life. If it is the case that the prosecution would fail without you – as did in fact happen with Moran, as you say – then why did Moriarty not think that he might safely return, stand his trial, and brazen it out, after he had killed you, assuming that he had succeeded in doing so?'

'I am sure that the possibility of doing so had occurred to him,' said Holmes. 'But remember that the smaller fry, those who made up the greater bulk of the gang, would be taken, and, more to the point convicted, for they worked more or less openly, they had not their master's genius, or opportunities, for concealment. And then, even if the case against Moriarty did fail without me – and, although probable, that was not by any means a cast-iron certainty, he might well have been convicted even without me, had there been a competent prosecuting attorney – still the police would mark him, and mark him well. Patterson and Lestrade knew almost as much about the gang as I did myself, though, since only I had carried out much of the investigation, the finer points as to the presentation of the evidence were beyond them. Scotland Yard would watch Moriarty so closely that he would never have the chance to build up new connections, to revive his evil empire. Let him but commit the most homely of nuisances under the railway arches at three in the morning, in the midst of a November fog, and there would be an inspector of detectives there to feel his collar.'

I laughed. 'Lestrade is tenacious enough, certainly. I am sure you are right.'

Holmes nodded. 'And they would make any charge stick, however trivial it may have been. Indeed, I am not at all sure that they would wait for him to offend before they charged him.'

'What, you don't mean they might falsify the evidence?'

'Aye, Watson, I mean just that. Reprehensible enough, to be sure, but I have often seen an odd light in Lestrade's eyes, a light betraying not merely anger but a desire for revenge at all costs, as the investigation was turned aside yet again for lack of any proofs, and months of work were frustrated. My own respect for the law is second to none, but I cannot swear that I would entirely blame Lestrade if he chose to interpret that law in favour of those innocents whom Moriarty fed upon. And even had he refrained from doing so, I had other friends in London, who would not have taken kindly to Moriarty's eliminating me. For instance, there was a certain Dr John Watson, who might have –'

'Indeed,' said I. 'Had the fellow shown his face here, I'd have –'

'To be sure you would. His life, in short, would have been intolerable.'

'And so Moriarty decided it was better to die, rather than live a hunted, haunted life of forced respectability, looking over his shoulder all the time. He was undoubtedly evil, but it is still rather sad, that, Holmes.'

Holmes laughed silently. 'Not at all, Watson. I assure you that nothing could have been further from his mind. He planned to kill me, and then resume his career, but not in England.'

'Indeed? That is more like sense. Perfectly understand-able. In France, perhaps? If, as you say, his web extended there, he would surely –'

Holmes waved a hand. 'It is certainly tempting to think so. But the French police, though deficient in many respects, have as much tenacity as Lestrade or Gregson when they have cause for suspicion. I had friends there, too, Dubuque and le Villard and the others, and a word from Scotland Yard to Paris would make France too hot for the professor. No, he had taken that into account, you may be sure. Moreover, his plans were, as ever, on a grand scale, as you will learn. Now, one thing that you must know at the outset is that before I called upon you that fateful day in 1891, I had been at Mycroft's rooms for the whole afternoon.'

'I believe I had recorded that fact in my published account.'

Holmes nodded. 'What you did not record, for the simple reason that I had not told you, is that I had a long talk with Mycroft before I called upon you.'

I raised an eyebrow. 'On a Friday afternoon? I thought our diligent government servants would be at their desks until early evening?'

Holmes laughed. 'Do not let Mycroft – Sir Mycroft, indeed, now – hear you say as much. No, in the ordinary way of things, Mycroft would be the last to leave the office, but he had much on his mind that day, and needed to think in peace. Hence the early return home, for even the Diogenes Club would not have given him the necessary quietness.'

'Oh?' said I, recollecting the sepulchral atmosphere of that strange establishment. 'It must have been a deep matter indeed on which he sought inspiration.'

'Oh, it was, I assure you. For some time, Mycroft had been receiving reports from his agents in India, concerning activity on the northern borders.'

'Russian activity?'

'Just so.'

'Nothing new in that, surely?' I said. 'Russia has sought to extend her influence into India since – since I don't know when.'

'Since 1807, to be precise,' said Holmes. 'It was in that year that Napoleon suggested to Tsar Alexander that France and Russia should join forces to invade India and dispossess Britain, whose influence had gradually extended over the sub-continent in the century since the death of Aurangzeb, last of the Mogul emperors.'

'There you are, then. I may not have the exact dates on the tip of my tongue, but I do know that Russia was forever sniffing at the northern borders of India when I was out there.'

Holmes nodded. 'True enough, and Mycroft would not normally have bothered too much about it. But there had been disturbing reports, unusual activity, and my brother could not see what significance, if any, might attach to that. Mycroft was eager to discuss the matter, to see what answers I might have for him, but I fear I had other, more pressing, things on my mind, so that I paid little attention to Mycroft's worries. He saw how things were with me, and went so far as to shelve his own questions for the time being, so that we might make those plans with which you are already familiar.'

'Arranging for the cab in which Mycroft drove me to the station, and the like?' said I.

'Exactly.'

'By the by, Holmes, I never asked you at the time, but how came it that Mycroft had such skill as a cabby?'

He waved a hand impatiently. 'In his youth, he was a four-in-hand driver of some note. Indeed, his record on the London to Brighton road remained unchallenged for a considerable time. But the question now is this concern of Mycroft's as to India.'

'Ah, yes, I interrupted your account of the talk with Mycroft.'

Holmes looked a trifle disconcerted. 'I had finished,' said he, with a touch of petulance, 'apart from telling you to note the circumstance, for it will be quite pertinent later.'

'I duly note it, Holmes.'

'When we left for France, then, I had no real aim in view, other than to stay out of harm's way until such time as I was called to give evidence against Moriarty and the others. But when I heard that Moriarty had escaped the net, things changed. At the outset, I honestly believed that he would simply try to kill me at all costs, even if it meant his own life – I, too, had slightly underestimated him. You know the result, our own wanderings through Switzerland, until we came to the Falls of the Reichenbach. It is there that the account that I originally gave you begins to differ some-what from the truth.' He leaned back in his chair and stretched out his legs before the fire, then recommenced his narrative.

3

A Reichenbach retrospective

Sherlock Holmes lay back in his chair, gazed at the ceiling – which, just as in the old days, was exceedingly dusty – in that introspective way of his, and commenced the following narrative.

When the young Swiss messenger arrived at the Reichenbach Falls with a note for you, my dear Watson (said he) I knew well enough from the very outset that there was no mysterious Englishwoman lying at death's door.

Ever since I had received the telegram from Patterson, who was, you may recall, the inspector in charge of the official police action against the Moriarty gang, telling me that the professor had escaped the net, I had been expecting some devilry, though I could not predict in what form it would occur. Still, I had been on the lookout for something – anything – out of the ordinary, and here it was.

You will ask, Watson, why I did not return with you, and thereby avoid the danger which I fully expected to arise as soon as you were out of sight.

Well, for one thing it was just possible that I might have been wrong, that there could indeed have been an unfortunate English lady whose last moments would be eased by your presence. If that were so, then of course nothing would be lost by letting you return alone.

If, as I suspected, rightly in the event, the note was a ruse to get me on my own, then it was safer – for you, I mean – to let you go, and for me to face the danger alone, lest Moriarty, growing weary of trying to distract you from my side, should decide to eliminate us both. Yes, old fellow, I know that you would not have thought twice about that, but I had to – if not for your sake, then for the sake of your wife.

No, it was safer to say nothing, to let you return, and to wait there myself until the professor should appear.

He did so, as soon as you were out of sight. Not alone, as I suggested when I saw you after that gap of three years, but in company with two of his criminal associates, both very large, and both of an extremely unpleasant appearance.

Moriarty himself was pointing a large and wicked-looking revolver at me. The other two men were unarmed, but still looked dangerous enough in all conscience.

'I had not expected so large a welcoming committee,' I said.

Moriarty inclined his head in a little bow of acknowledgement. 'I fear that changed circumstances – which I deplore as much as you do – make it impossible for me to accord you all those courtesies, those personal attentions, shall we say, which I would have wished,' said he. 'This foolishness has gone on quite long enough, as I'm sure you will agree. There must be no room for mistakes this time, Holmes, hence the presence of my two colleagues.'

'May I at least leave a note for Watson?' I asked. 'He will be concerned enough about me as it is, without the added distress of not knowing exactly what may have occurred.'

Moriarty shook his head. 'I regret that it will not –' he broke off, and looked beyond me, towards the Falls, his eyes darting here and there, until they settled on the damp and slippery track that led to the edge and a curious light came into them – 'on second thoughts, perhaps I might permit it, but you will please be prudent as to what you write, for I fear that I must insist upon reading the finished product.'

'I had expected nothing else,' said I, and proceeded to write the note which you, Watson, later found and later still made public. I deliberately kept it non-committal in tone, for I knew that Moriarty had some scheme in mind. Reading your account later, I was struck by the fact that he had let me refer to the files of evidence against the gang, but then I realized that he intended to sacrifice his old friends – or at any rate to leave them to sink or swim as they could – the better to cover his own disappearance.

When I had finished, and Moriarty had read and approved my note, I placed it by the side of the path, weighted down with my cigarette case. 'My thanks for that civility,' I told Moriarty. 'I trust it will make Watson's mind somewhat easier.'

'Let us hope so. And now,' said he, looking at one of his henchmen, 'I think it is time to say farewell to Mr Holmes, if you would be so kind.'

The fellow looked at the slippery path, and the rushing torrent, with no great enthusiasm. 'Be quick,' urged the professor.

'I had thought, Professor, that perhaps you and I –?' I suggested.

'Dear me, Mr Holmes! Dear me, as I have had occasion to remark to you before.' He stared at me, an evil glint in his eye, like some sort of venomous reptile.

'Ah, yes,' said I. 'The little affair at Birlstone, as I recall.'

'I fooled you completely there, Holmes,' said Moriarty with a good deal of malicious satisfaction apparent in his voice. 'I had been commissioned to advise as to the elimination of Mr Douglas, only to see the job hopelessly bungled by a self-proclaimed expert assassin.' His head oscillated violently with emotion. 'Heaven preserve us from these amateurs of crime, whether American or home-grown! When he had made an absolute hash of a perfectly simple task, it was then, of course, quite necessary for me to flush Douglas out of hiding and so enable my own agents to complete the job, and who better to undertake that mundane, yet essential, task than the renowned Sherlock Holmes?'

'Hence the curious message, with the vital words written clearly, and only the trivial statements in cipher?'

'Quite so. I knew it could not fail to arouse your curiosity.'

'I was aware there was something odd about a cipher message of which the essential elements, the very elements which should have been secret, were not in cipher and thus no secret, but I confess I did not suspect that,' said I. 'But as to this present difference of opinion, I had expected that it would be man to man, if the phrase is not entirely inapplicable in the circumstances.'

Moriarty's eyes glittered angrily at the insult. 'You are, what, thirty-five years old? I am nearer sixty than fifty, and not in the best of condition, having led a somewhat sedentary, though reasonably exciting, life. Besides,' he added, a curious note of exaltation in his voice, 'I must conserve my strength. For the mountains, you understand, Holmes. Yes, the mountains.' There was a strange gleam in his eye as he spoke, and that along with his tone made me think rapidly.

I glanced up at the peaks around us. 'It is a little early in the season for comfort.'

Moriarty laughed heartily. 'These anthills? Merely practice, I assure you. But useful practice, nonetheless. And now, enough of this tomfoolery.' He gestured towards the Falls with the muzzle of the revolver. 'Let us get it over and done with.'

The man whom he had indicated as my executioner

seemed disposed to dispute matters. 'Why couldn't you shoot him and have done?' he asked, a reasonable enough question, I thought, seen from his viewpoint.

'Fool!' hissed Moriarty. 'It must look like an accident, and how could it do that if he had a bullet in him? Finish the job now, and be quick, before that obstinate clown of a doctor returns.'

The fellow stepped forward, motioning me to go ahead of him along the path to the edge of the Falls. I walked slowly, ostensibly because the wet earth made it dangerous to hasten, but in reality that I might have a chance to speak to the man who edged his way gingerly along behind me.

'You are aware that Moriarty will not let you return?' said I. 'He could, as you say, have shot me with impunity, for a body going over the Falls is unlikely ever to be recovered for a close examination as to the presence or absence of bullet holes.'

'What on earth are you talking about?' said he – or words to that general effect, for he was a coarse fellow.

'It is not in the least a matter of making my death look accidental,' I went on, 'but rather of making it look as if Moriarty had perished along with me. In that way, nobody will think to look for him among those mountains of which he spoke just now. It is surely patently obvious that such a plan can only succeed if there are two lines of footprints going to the very edge of the Falls – and, by the way, we have reached that edge now – but none going back?'

My companion, who was practically clinging to the wall of rock, hesitated, and looked back at the tracks we had left.

'You take my point?' I said.

He gazed back along the path at Moriarty, as if seeking inspiration from his master. Moriarty called out something, but it was lost in the crashing of the Falls. As if to reinforce his instructions, the professor raised his revolver, and fired a single shot, which took a chip out of the rock a yard above our heads.

'He wants the job finished,' said my companion, evidently a man of few words and little imagination, but capable of grasping one central theme, if it were made clear to him.

'That is true enough, but —' before I could reason further with him, he had made up his mind, and made a hesitant sort of charge at me.

I have said that he was a big man. And yet he was cautious, his charge when he made it was hesitant, for he was afraid for his life. The path was narrow and damp, unsafe even for men not engaged in a hand-to-hand struggle. Moreover, he believed, where I did not, that the professor would permit him to return in safety.

On the other hand, I had nothing to lose, for I knew that the professor would not, could not, allow either me or my assailant to leave there alive, whatever might be the outcome of the little contest at the end of the path.

I met the reluctant attack confidently, then, with a grip which I had seen demonstrated some years previously by a member of the Japanese Legation, a nobleman who was an adept in the secret art of baritsu, a wrestling technique so secret that few of the Japanese themselves are aware of its existence.

I managed to catch my assailant off balance, and turn his charge. He twisted round on the slippery path, overbalanced, and groped frantically at the air for what seemed an eternity. Then he let out a hideous scream, and went over the edge.

And so did I.

I, too, had lost my footing on the damp ledge, and although I had evaded my attacker's grasp easily enough, over I went. I was more fortunate than Moriarty's poor dupe, inasmuch as I did not fall outwards into the torrent, but rather slipped over and downwards, and was thus able to clutch at the edge of the path as I went. My fingers found some slight purchase, and I clutched at it for dear life, in the most literal sense. My arms felt as if they had been pulled from their sockets, but I held on, and hung there by my fingertips, my feet kicking out over the Falls.

My position was far from being an enviable one, to put it mildly indeed. The waters rushed and crashed at my side, while the final scream of the poor wretch I had sent to his death still echoed in my ears, a reminder of the fate which almost certainly awaited me.

Worse still, I had the horrid sensation that my hands were slipping from the moist rock. To this day, I cannot say whether it was imagination, or whether it was literally true, I only know that I fully expected to end my life at any second in the raging Falls.

I kicked desperately at the rock face, and my boots encountered something in the nature of a tiny ledge, or crevice, so that I was able to gain some purchase with one foot, and that gave me new heart.

Cautiously, I moved the other foot along and up, until I was able to find another hold. After that, it was a matter of levering myself up, an inch at a time, always fearful that my hands would slip back, or that the professor would see my efforts, and send a bullet towards me.

Time seemed to stand still. It felt as if it were hours, but it cannot have been more than five minutes, ten at most, before I scrambled up the last few inches and collapsed, sobbing from sheer exhaustion, on the path. Yet there was no sign of Moriarty or the other villain who had accompanied him.

I realized at once that they had seen the two of us go over, and thinking, quite logically under the circumstances, that we were both lost in the torrent, they had made good their escape.

It was at this point that I thought out what I should do next, exactly as I said when I saw you in 1894, Watson, though my thoughts were not quite along the lines that I was obliged to suggest then.

As soon as he had said it, I had immediately connected the professor's mention of mountains, compared with which the Swiss Alps were anthills, with Mycroft's earlier concern as to the northern borders of India -

'One moment,' I interrupted.

Sherlock Holmes looked at me with some vexation.

'I am sorry to break the flow of so riveting a narrative,' said I, 'but I really must ask if you had made that connection as rapidly as you claim.'

'I had,' said he. 'Surely it was not so very difficult? Mycroft had told me that there was trouble brewing in the Himalaya, and here was Moriarty looking forward to a sojourn in the mountains. Where is the mystery there?'

'Well,' said I laughing, 'I have known men who would not have made the connection quite so readily.'

Holmes leaned forward, and gazed earnestly at me. 'You still fail to get the full measure of Moriarty, Doctor,' said he. 'His ideas were on a grand scale, greater even than those of the late and unlamented Baron Maupertuis. I had made England too hot to hold him, and the official police would do the same for most of the countries of Europe. Moriarty therefore looked further afield, it was as simple as that.'

'But – but – what you are suggesting is fantastic! Do you really mean that Moriarty fancied himself as – what – Emperor of India?'

Holmes nodded gravely. 'Is it so improbable? He would only be doing what the present viceroy does, after all. I believe he would have made a good ruler, within his limits, for his organizational ability was second to none. In the event of insurrection, he would have had the Russian army at his disposal, and in return for all this he would merely have to guarantee the Russians access to the warm water ports. What is so very strange about that? Remember that if the Russians had occupied India a century ago, as they thought of doing, they would not have done anything very different from that, beyond putting in one of their own men as governor.'

'Even so, Holmes.'

'And then Moriarty, as a Englishman, would be better able to gain the confidence of the native princelings, used to English overlords as they were, than a Russian. It was masterly.'

'But to betray his country in that fashion!'

Holmes gazed over my shoulder. 'I am sure that Moriarty simply did not see matters in that light. He was devoid of all moral scruples. His loyalties were, and always had been, solely to himself, and anything or anyone who got in the way of his ambitions had to be removed.'

'I see. And having worked all this out at Reichenbach, you decided that it was more important to pursue Moriarty than to return to London and ensure the conviction of the others?'

Holmes nodded. 'There was no comparison. I had hopes that the police and the prosecution might secure convictions without me, as indeed they did for the most part. But it would have been better to let the entire gang go free than to permit their leader to continue with his evil career. All that came to me as I lay there, recovering my breath.'

'So why did you not wait there until I returned? We might have tracked him down together, Holmes.'

He slapped my back. 'Good old Watson! But I had to think of your wife, you know. She had never openly objected to our little jaunts together, but I had seen the look in her eyes whenever you left your comfortable home. When you were obliged to be away for a couple of weeks together at the time of that little affair at Baskerville Hall, she was positively short-spoken with me when next I saw her. Moreover, it would be very useful to me if the professor thought that I was in fact dead.'

'I see. And the watcher on the cliff above, then, the man you thought was Colonel Moran? What about him?'

Holmes made an impatient gesture. 'I knew it could not be Moran, for of course I knew he had been arrested. I only said it was Moran later, to confuse the issue – and quite successfully, as it appears. The fact that the man on top of the cliff was obliged to roll boulders down upon me indicated that he had no better weapon, which also ruled Moriarty out, for he was armed. It must therefore be the second of the two men who had accompanied Moriarty. I assume that he had originally been left behind to confirm that you and the other searchers came to the correct conclusion – correct from Moriarty's point of view, that is – that the professor and I had gone into the Falls together.'

'And he tried to finish the job his ruffianly mate had started?'

Holmes nodded. 'Just so. He evidently had some misplaced notion of loyalty to Moriarty, though Heaven only knows why. Now, when I realized that the second man knew that I was not dead, I was in something of a quandary. It would, as I say, have been very useful if Moriarty thought he was rid of me; he would not be so much on his guard if he believed me to be dead. On the other hand, if he knew I was still alive, that knowledge would make my pursuit of him that much harder, but it did not in the least alter the fact that such a pursuit was still necessary, indeed essential. I had some slight hopes that the watcher might have been instructed to return to London, and not continue the journey with Moriarty, and in the event that is what happened, so that the professor did not learn of my escape until later.'

'And the rest of your journey was broadly as you told me?'

'It was. I did my forced march over the mountains, and got on to Moriarty's track at the Swiss border, being relieved to discover that he had been alone, which meant that the watcher had returned to London, and therefore that I was comparatively safe. I had, of course, sufficient funds, for you will recall that I had our letter of credit in my pocket –'

'I do recall it,' said I. 'I had cause to regret that I had allowed you to hold our money, for I was obliged to borrow a trifling sum from the British Consul, and take the cheapest route back to London. And I may add that it was not a particularly enjoyable voyage, though it was memorable. In the last stages, going through France, I was compelled to exist on stale baguettes and an offensively rank cheese made from goat's milk.'

'You have my deepest sympathy,' said Holmes, though I regret to record that his face showed distinct signs of badly suppressed laughter. 'Still, it was unavoidable. And I am certain you have made up for any gastronomic deficiencies since then. When I arrived at Florence I sent a telegram to Mycroft, and he replied by coming to meet me.'

'Jupiter descending, indeed!' said I.

Holmes laughed. 'It was a somewhat unusual occurrence, but then it was a somewhat unusual combination of events which had caused it. As luck would have it, the international situation was relatively calm at the time – although even then Mycroft absolutely assured me later that the Panama Canal scandal might have been largely averted had he been on hand to send a note of no more than four lines to the French Ambassador. Still, these things cannot always be helped. As it was, we were able to discuss the more urgent matter quite thoroughly, and to make our plans accordingly. And, to cut a long story short, in a day or so I was heading for Port Said and Colombo, a route with which you are already familiar from your service in Afghanistan, with my ultimate destination being India. It is at that point that the journals of Major Dyce begin.'

PART TWO

From the journal of Lieutenant (later Major) Harold Dyce, of the Indian Army Cartographic Service

4

Darjeeling

I had spent the winter of 1890 in the plains, doing a survey of one of the native principalities, before returning to Calcutta late in the spring of '91 for further orders. The previous summer, I had been doing some mapping in the high mountains, almost as far as the border with Tibet – I could not remain there in winter, for travel in the higher mountains is only possible during the short summers – and I had fallen in love with the high peaks, so I had hopes that I might be sent there again.

In Calcutta, I was somewhat surprised to be ordered to report to a Captain Gerald Fenton, a man whom I had never met. I went along to his office, and found him seated at a large desk which was covered all over with maps and papers, to a depth of a couple of inches. Fenton was a short, wiry man with a thin, dark moustache and a heavily tanned skin. Exchange his uniform for a white dhoti, and he could pass for almost any of the indigenous races of southern India.

This was an enormous asset in his work, for I soon learned that he was one of that curious breed called Political Officers, who are entrusted with the secret work of the army and of the government in India, and that he often found it advisable to disguise himself, in order to move about undetected.

He passed me a crumpled paper packet containing the pungent native cigarettes, lighting one for himself as he did so.

'No, thank you,' I told him. 'I have always thought they should be proffered only to very good friends, or to mortal enemies.'

Fenton laughed. 'Perhaps you are right.' He sat up in his chair, and became serious. 'Now, I understand from your commanding officer that you have some knowledge of the area towards the Tibetan border?'

I explained that I had done some cartographic work there the previous year, Fenton listening in silence as I spoke.

When I had done, he said, 'We have had some disturbing reports of Russian activity in Tibet itself. I have spent some time in that region, and speak some Tibetan, and therefore I have been ordered to look into the reports, to evaluate how great the actual danger might be. Would you have any objection to coming along with me? There may be a chance of doing some mapping, though that must necessarily be secondary to our main task.'

'I should be delighted,' said I.

Fenton looked worried. 'There may well be some danger,' he said.

'So much the better!'

The worried look vanished. 'I had hopes you would say as much. Now, we shall need to disguise ourselves, for Tibet, as you will know, is forbidden to foreigners. In the past I have been both a merchant and a pilgrim in those parts. A merchant can take mules, bearers and the like, and hence plenty of supplies, but cannot stray too far from the main centres of population. A pilgrim must travel light, but then a pilgrim is not obliged to stick to the highroads, so I think we shall be Indian Buddhists, visiting the sacred sites. What say you to that?'

'I have some knowledge of Urdu and Hindi,' said I, 'so I ought to be able to pass all but the most rigorous examination.'

'Excellent. I propose to include two old acquaintances of mine in the party, both of whom should be very useful to us.' It was said in a cheerful enough tone, but he seemed to hesitate.

I asked, 'Was there something more?'

Fenton rummaged amongst the litter of papers on his desk, and held up a lengthy telegram. 'London is, as you will readily imagine, quite concerned at the news of any possible increase in Russian activity in those parts,' he said. 'They are actually thinking of sending their own representative.' He raised an expressive eyebrow. 'Still, if it is some portly gentleman from the FO, we can always pass him on to the colonel, to be shown round the barracks and given a good dinner before he sets off for home again. So that should not detain us unduly.'

'When do you intend to start?' I asked.

'The Governor and his staff will be moving to Darjeeling very soon,' said Fenton. 'We shall go along with them, so that we do not draw undue attention to ourselves. It does mean a slight delay, but it may be worth it for the concealment it will afford us – we cannot be sure that we are not observed, even here. My two colleagues are already in Darjeeling, and will have the necessary preparations all complete by the time we arrive, so that we can leave at once, or at any rate as soon as our government inspector has arrived, assuming that he ever does, and assuming further that he wants to talk to us before we go, because you know how these fellows work. They come along, make polite noises to the generals and colonels, have a quick look round, then clear off back home without talking to the men on the ground.'

I nodded agreement to this, and left, to make my own simple preparations, and to say my own farewells, few in number though they were. Not that I dislike my fellow man, much less my fellow woman, but the nature of my work had always meant that I had few opportunities to make any real lasting friendships.

A week or two later, Fenton and I were on the little railway that runs to the hill town of Darjeeling, whose name is familiar to every grocer and tea drinker in England.

The entire machinery of government decamps from Calcutta to Darjeeling each summer, to escape the stifling heat and humidity of the coast. Because of this regular influx of British society, Darjeeling is a microcosm of England. There are place names like The Dingle or The Shrubbery, and flowers that would not disgrace any park in Cheltenham. The children attend St Paul's School, or worship in St Andrew's Church, and there is no shortage of revelry of a night, when officers from the British regiment stationed there dine and dance with the daughters of the various government officials, or with those enterprising ladies who travel from England for the express purpose of finding husbands.

But Fenton assured me as we sat on the little train that there would be little time for these civilized amenities, for we must complete our preparations and be off as soon as may be.

When we arrived at Darjeeling, however, the station master had a telegram for Fenton. He ripped it open, and read it with a darkening brow. 'Damn!'

'Well?'

He took my arm and steered me away from the throng on the platform. 'The FO are sending their own man, as I had feared,' said he in a low tone. 'We are to wait until he arrives – he is on his way now, apparently – and take him along with us.'

'Wonderful. A morocco-bound mandarin will be an excellent companion in the high passes.'

Fenton's face cleared. 'It may never come to that. We shall take him to Observatory Hill, show him the panoramic view of the Himalaya, and ask if he feels quite up to doing his twenty miles a day with us.'

'Are we up to twenty miles a day ourselves, I wonder?'

'Hardly,' said Fenton with a wry grin. 'Two miles a day will be excellent progress in some of the places we may be obliged to visit. But an armchair adventurer, whose only glory and triumph consists of having once taken third place in the Hansard Handicap, is hardly likely to know that. No, what really concerns me is that if we have to hang about here waiting for this fellow to show up, we shall miss part of the season for travelling in the mountains. Still, orders is orders, as we know to our cost. And I fear that our orders are quite specific: we are to give this fellow every possible assistance, whatever strange requests he may make. And now, by way of some compensation for this annoyance, let me cheer you up by introducing you to our companions.'

Fenton had a bungalow on the outskirts of town, somewhat away from the bulk of the population, in order, he said, that he might come and go unobserved that much easier. I would stay there with him, and the two men who were to go with us were there already.

The first man was Ram Dass, a short, nondescript Indian of indeterminate age, one of the famous 'pundits'. These were Indians who did mapping and exploration work along the northern borders, on behalf of the British government. Incredibly brave and hardy men, between them they were responsible for producing almost every one of the excellent maps of these remote areas. In return, they were poorly paid, their work seldom praised or even recognized save by their immediate superiors, and they ran a very good chance of dying violent and lonely deaths on some remote hillside.

The other man was called Thupten Norbu, as near as I can render it. He was a Tibetan, very tall, over six feet in height, and thin, his features nearer the Chinese than the Indian, and he was invariably dressed in a long orange robe. He spoke Tibetan, along with English and many of the Indian languages, and he would be our guide, and our interpreter when needed, although both Fenton and Dass spoke some Tibetan – though Norbu declared himself far from satisfied with either of their accents.

In the week or so that followed my arrival, Norbu told me something of the state of Tibet at that time. Nominally the country was under the control of the Chinese emperors, but that control was weak, partly because of the great distance of isolated Tibet from the Chinese capital, partly because China herself was decadent, in a fair way to being torn apart by internal strife.

The great powers, said Norbu wryly, were by no means unwilling to see this disintegration of China, for it presented them with the opportunity to extend their own influence into that vast marketplace. All of them – Britain included – were engaged in this reprehensible practice. Britain, indeed, had fought some disgraceful wars in order not only to compel the Chinese to buy opium from British merchants, but to pay compensation for their effrontery in daring to object to the trade in the first place.

More to the immediate purpose, Russia had occupied Chinese territory north of the Amur, and more or less compelled the Chinese to legalize the seizure by signing a treaty at Peking in 1860. This region was quite close to the northern border of Tibet, so it was by no means fanciful to suppose that Russia would move quickly to fill the gap left by a collapse of Chinese influence. It was absolutely necessary that Russia should gain control of those countries to the north of India – Tibet, Afghanistan and the like – before she could make any attempt to move into India itself.

The lamas who ruled Tibet had no particular love for their Chinese overlords, Norbu went on, and would not be too sorry to see them leave, but there was some debate as to what would, or should, happen thereafter. Some Tibetans wanted to rule themselves, but most of them realized that Tibet's significant position in between British India and Russia made that impossible for all practical purposes. Some, therefore, inclined to an alliance with Britain, but equally some favoured Russia. This was the problem to which Fenton – and his opposite numbers on the Russian general staff, of course – must endeavour to find a solution.

We spent a few days deciding what equipment we should take – it was not very elaborate, for we should be obliged to carry it all on our backs – and making plans as to the best route to take.

Once that was done, we were obliged to possess our souls in patience, waiting for the man the Foreign Office would send. I did not find the waiting too unwelcome, for I was able to meet some of those ladies who, as I have said, made Darjeeling a very pleasant place for a young army officer to be stationed. I attended more dances in a few weeks there than I had in all my previous time in India, and so had few complaints.

Fenton, however, fretted very badly over the delay, saying that the year was getting on, the summer would be over before we could take our leave, and the like. In vain did I try to advise him to enjoy the comforts of civilization while he could. He invariably heard me out with ill-concealed impatience, swore in an unmannerly fashion, then set off for a walk or a ride among the hills.

And then one day Fenton, greatly elated, opened a telegram over breakfast, and told me that our visitor should be arriving on the little train due into Darjeeling that very morning. We strolled along to the station with no great enthusiasm, determined to talk our visitor out of accompanying us if we possibly could, for we both felt sure he would prove something of a liability. On the other hand, we felt happier that, one way or another, we should soon be off, for we had already been compelled to delay our departure quite long enough.

'Have you ever crossed the border into Tibet?' Fenton asked me, as we sat smoking in the little waiting room, he with one of his infernal Indian gaspers in his mouth, I with a relatively decent lunkah.

'Never. I was tempted to try doing so last year, I was near the border, but I had strict orders to stay this side.'

Fenton nodded. 'Unwise to cross unless you are disguised, and have some object in view,' said he. His voice grew reflective. 'It is a curious country. For some strange reason, far more boys are born than girls.' He looked round the waiting room, which was empty save for us, and then lowered his voice anyway. 'Accordingly, the same wife usually has more than one husband, often marrying all the brothers from one family.'

'Indeed? I have come across men who maintained more than one establishment – though I hasten to say that I have never been tempted to emulate them – but I cannot recall ever meeting a woman who behaved in that fashion.'

'Unusual, is it not? And apparently even that proves unequal to the task of absorbing all the surplus men, so that about half the male population are celibate monks. The country is run by the lamas, a cross between priests and witch-doctors, and the people are more superstitious than the Irish peasantry.'

'And that is the sort of benighted place you would bring under the umbrella of the Empire?'

'Yes, as a buffer to protect the north of India.' Fenton waved a hand to indicate the station, the town, and the hills beyond. 'We are two days from Tibet, here. Would you like to see the Imperial Russian eagle flying from the flagpole yonder? Tibet is the key that would unlock India for the Tsar.' He rose and crushed his cigarette end beneath his heel. 'The train is here.'

We had, of course, no idea as to what our visitor from London might look like, or even what his name was, so we had to wait on the little platform until the tea-planters, army men and ICS officials had departed.

One man remained on the platform, and I had grown so used to the notion of the FO sending some superannuated clerk – for Fenton and I had talked so often about him that we had constructed our own unflattering picture of him, down to the fussily buttoned gaiters on the pudgy little feet – that for a moment I did not realize that this must be our man.

He reminded me irresistibly of Norbu, being as tall as the Tibetan, as thin, and looking every bit as ascetic. His eyes were set close together, and his great hooked nose was like the beak of some curious mountain bird. He cast an extraordinarily penetrating glance at Fenton and myself, before coming towards us, and saying, 'Captain Fenton?'

'I'm Gerald Fenton, and this is Lieutenant Harold Dyce. You, I take it, are the gentleman we were expecting from London?'

'I am. My name is Sigerson.'

Fenton raised an eyebrow, but held out his hand.

'It is a Norwegian name,' explained Sigerson, in perfect English without the slightest hint of any accent.

'Indeed?' said Fenton, rank disbelief in his voice. 'And

how was Oslo, last time you saw it? Not vastly different from London, I should judge?'

Sigerson laughed, in a peculiar, silent fashion. 'Well,' said he, 'one name is as good as another. As Chandra Dass, or Mr Patak Singh, might well tell you.'

I could see a look of respect dawn in Fenton's eyes. 'You know a great deal, Mr Sigerson.'

Sigerson nodded. 'It is quite essential that I should impress you at the outset, gentlemen. You see, I am being very frank with you, for I absolutely need your co-operation, and I am well aware that you must resent having my presence thus cavalierly thrust upon you.'

Of course, Fenton and I protested that he was quite wrong, that such a thought had not entered our heads, that it would not, and indeed could not, ever do so.

Sigerson heard us out, then said, 'It would be curious if you did not resent my presence here. In your place, I should do the same. And I might as well say at the very outset that my name is nothing like Sigerson. However, there are one or two Scandinavian explorers in this region at present, and it suits my present purposes to be thought of as one of them. Now, having cleared that little matter up it is, I assure you, quite essential that I get into Tibet as soon as possible.'

'We are all ready,' said Fenton, with no sign of annoyance, much to my surprise. 'We have only been waiting until you should arrive.'

'I apologize for the delay,' said Sigerson. 'I got here as soon as humanly possible, but it is a long journey, as you are well aware.'

'And you positively insist upon going into Tibet in person?' Fenton asked him.

'It is, as I say, essential. Not that I imply any lack of confidence in either of you, but I know the enemy we are pursuing, and you do not.'

'The Russian agent?' said Fenton, in a low tone.

Sigerson laughed. 'Hardly.' He picked up a shabby suit-case from the platform. 'If you would be so kind as to provide me with a drink of something cool, and perhaps an armchair, I shall explain how matters stand.'

5

A Norwegian named Sigerson

The man who called himself Sigerson accepted a brandy and soda from Fenton, and sat back in a chair on the veranda overlooking the distant sweep of hills. The rest of us, curious as to what he might have to say, gathered around him in silence.

'Thank you,' said he, taking a drink from his glass. 'And now, I feel that some explanation is necessary as to why you have been burdened with my company in this somewhat brusque fashion.'

Naturally we made the customary polite noises, but Sigerson waved a hand, and went on, 'You will be well aware that Russia has, for many years, been looking to extend her influence into Tibet, and thence into India. You may also know that recent reports indicate an increase of Russian activity in that area, and that is something which the government in London take very seriously.'

Fenton nodded. 'We had heard all that.'

'What you do not know,' Sigerson went on, 'is that I have reason – excellent reason – to believe that an Englishman is involved with the Russian activity.'

Fenton and myself expressed some surprise at this, as may be readily imagined.

Sigerson heard us out, then said, 'It is difficult to believe, I know. But if you knew this villain as well as I do, you would perhaps not find it quite so hard to accept.'

'Who is he, then?' I asked. 'Or is that a secret?'

Sigerson thought for a moment, then smiled. 'I am asking you to run a great risk, so it is perhaps only right that I should trust you to some extent,' said he. 'I do not imagine that the name will mean anything to you, but it is a – a gentleman – named Moriarty.'

I shook my head, for the name meant nothing to me.

Fenton frowned, though, as if in thought, then said, 'It could not be Professor James Moriarty that you mean?'

'It is none other,' said Sigerson, a curious expression crossing his face. 'You know of him, then?'

'I know the man himself,' said Fenton, unexpectedly. 'Or I did, rather, for he coached me for the army entrance exams, years ago. You are way off the mark there though, I fear, Mr Sigerson. Why, a more inoffensive old chap could hardly be imagined! He was, if anything, somewhat of a figure of fun amongst the candidates whom he coached – did you know that his brother is also called James? We used to laugh about that – strictly amongst ourselves, though, for the professor had something of a way with him. He seldom, if ever, actually lost his temper, but you knew well enough when he was displeased. He had a way of making his disappointment known, if you follow me.'

'I am aware of the fact,' said Sigerson drily. 'As, indeed, many of those who have crossed the professor have been made aware of it – too late. I could give you the names of at least a dozen men who have met very unpleasant deaths after falling foul of Moriarty, and I have not the slightest doubt that there are many more unknown to me.'

I started to say something, I forget what it may have been, but Fenton raised a hand. 'There was always something a little odd – perhaps even sinister – about him, that's true,' he said thoughtfully. 'And yet what you suggest is staggering in its enormity. That any Englishman could act in such a fashion!'

'Moriarty's loyalties are, and always have been, very much to himself,' said Sigerson, in a matter-of-fact tone. 'Did you never bother to query why he, who had been a professor, should have ended up coaching young men for the army entrance examinations? After all, laudable though the profession of army coach may be, and delightful company as I am sure you all were, it was not exactly the usual course of a brilliant academic career.'

'There was some talk,' agreed Fenton, 'some scurrilous rumours, to which most of us attached very little truth.'

'I suspect that they understated the facts,' said Sigerson. 'He seemed set for a brilliant academic career, but he could not hide his true nature, and drifted irresistibly into a life of crime. At the same time as he was, ostensibly, that "inoffensive old chap" whom you knew so well, he was the organizing genius behind most of the large-scale criminal activity in London, aye, and outside London as well, of late. His tentacles ran everywhere, even into the highest reaches of the London police force, and the courts, if my assumptions are correct. His regiment of rogues was as well drilled, as well supplied, as the Guards, and twice as strong in terms of numbers.'

Fenton looked grave. 'He had some expensive pictures and the like in his lodgings, that is certain,' he said. 'I often wondered where he got the money, for his personal tastes seemed ascetic in the extreme, and the fees he garnered from his pupils were not munificent.'

'The wages of sin can be impressive, for a time at least,' said Sigerson sententiously.

'Well, then,' said Fenton. 'Supposing – and I am still not entirely convinced – but supposing for one moment that your suggestions are correct, still, the professor is not a particularly young man, and scarcely fitted for a long campaign in the mountains.'

'He may be fitter than we might think,' said Sigerson. 'And besides, there are mules, porters, surely? You would know more as to that than I.'

'There have been some remarkable feats of exploration by the least likely adventurers,' I pointed out.

'Now, what I need from you at this point is an expert view of what Moriarty and his Russian accomplices might have in mind,' said Sigerson. 'You know the situation here at first hand, and I do not. Let us start from the premise that a determined man wished to aid the Russians in their attempt to wrest control of Tibet from the present administration. How would he go about it?'

'Norbu is better qualified to answer that than I,' said Fenton, looking at the tall Tibetan. Both Norbu and Dass were listening intently to our conversation. They would run the same risks as the rest of us, so it was only fair that they should know as much as we did. Those distinctions between the races which seem so important in the Club at Simla or Ootie prove less significant when you are looking death in the face, and only a friend, be the colour of his skin what it may, can be of assistance to you.

'Ultimately, any such project could only work if the parties concerned had the approval of the lamas,' Norbu told us. 'If that were not the case, then an invader must be prepared to impose strict military rule on the country.'

'Yet the Chinese do not seem to have too much difficulty?' said Fenton.

Norbu smiled. 'Although we may assert our independence – and have done for a thousand years – yet the Chinese and the Tibetans share common ancestors, and have much in common, the languages and the cultures being broadly similar. Then the Chinese permit us to

an, then, or a diplomat,' mused Sigerson. 'Or
, a military attaché at one of their embassies
An eye for the route an invading army must
he knowledge of the politenesses of an ambas-
s some grasp of the Tibetan language. Yes, he
e shape, this adversary of ours, albeit the shape
s one. What is certain is that his ally, Moriarty,
ermined, and a most dangerous man. And they
where? Lhasa?'

oked puzzled. 'Lhasa is certainly the seat of
y country,' he agreed. 'However, there are vari-
cations. The spiritual head of Tibet is the Dalai
he is in Lhasa, the seat of government, that
rue. However, the present incarnation of His
s a young boy, who must be trained in the ordi-
of life. Until His Holiness is old enough to
s proper place, the power is in the hands of the

understand,' said Sigerson. 'So that any negotia-
t needs be done with this Regent?'
nodded vigorously. 'And that is one of the compli-
said he. 'The Regent is the Abbot of the monas-
en-gye-ling, and he is no lover of the Russians. So
zzled as to what these Russians can hope to achieve.
now of the Regent's antipathy to Russia, they must
ey are wasting their time. If not, then they are very
and are in for a grave disappointment.'

l, then!' said Fenton, rubbing his hands together. 'It
seem that we have little need for concern, or indeed
te. If our Russian friends – and the professor, if
he has anything to do with it, which is still not
– do get there ahead of us, then they'll be sent
g with the proverbial flea in their ear.'
erson shook his head slowly. 'It might be fatal – in a

govern ourselves, or at any rate permit us that illusion. An invading army of obvious foreigners, determined to rule by force, might not find things quite so straightforward.'

'You are postulating some sort of formal treaty, then?' asked Sigerson.

Norbu nodded gravely. 'That would be the safest, simplest way to approach things,' said he. 'You must understand that there are various factions amongst the Tibetan authorities, some favouring Russia, some Britain – some, indeed, would like the Chinese overlordship to continue. My own sympathies will be clear to you, but you should know that each of the foreign powers has its own lobby.'

Dass, who had seemed restless for some time as he listened, now leaned over to Fenton, and muttered something in a hoarse whisper, using a language I could not recognize.

Fenton gave a slight start. 'By Jove, I think Dass is right!' He sat upright in his chair, and gazed earnestly at Sigerson. 'As you will guess, we have our own agents, our own informants, who keep as close a watch on the Russians as may be – just as they keep watch on us, if we are careless enough to let them.' He stared out at the distant Himalaya. 'It is a curious profession, this of ours,' he said. 'The one-eyed beggar whom you kick out of your way, the evil-smelling dealer in horses or gatherer of night-soil whom you cross the road to avoid, may report directly to the office of the viceroy, and hold the future of a half-dozen kingdoms and principalities in his grimy paws.'

Sigerson laughed. 'I had thought that my own trade was an odd one, but I see I was wrong,' said he – but I noticed that he took good care not to say what that trade might be.

Fenton went on, 'One of our men in Russia, a very brave man, who daily runs the risk of certain and hideous death if he is discovered, sent a report some while ago, at the

beginning of spr
outfitted to move
but that the expe
the odd facts whic
not been able to ex
your man, my old t
sor, which I still beg
the delay. They have
as we were obliged t

Sigerson nodded.
Moriarty had got wor
did. I had made some
find that he had ente
Russia, though, he wo
Europe. Yes, I think yo
more of this expedition?

Fenton shook his head
won at great risk,' said he
Prince Exe.'

'Exe?' I said, puzzled. I
knew that many members o
ually spoke French, but it s

Fenton laughed at my be
cross in the air. '"X," the un
braic problems the professor
'We must call him that, for v
him.'

'Yet he is an aristocrat?' said

'A prince, which in Russia
thing. "Prince," with them, is no
but a distinction conferred upo
certain rank in the army, or seni
approximates most closely to th
practical purposes,' said Fenton d

'An army n
possibly both
or legations.
take, and son
sador. Perha
begins to tal
is a nebulou
is a most de
are bound –

Norbu l
power in m
ous compli
Lama, and
much is t
Holiness i
nary ways
assume h
Regent.'

'I quit
tions mu

Norbu
cations,'
tery of T
I am puz
If they
know t
foolish

'Wel
would
for ha
indeed
prove
packi
Sig

quite literal sense – to underestimate Moriarty,' he said. Then, to Norbu, 'You say the Regent is no friend of Russia. Does that mean that he might lean towards Britain, think you?'

'He would see Tibet free, I think – as would I,' said Norbu. 'But if it is between Britain and Russia, then I think Britain would have the advantage.'

'What are you driving at, Mr Sigerson?' I asked.

'Well, does it not strike you that one possibility is that the professor – a trained teacher – might offer to tutor the young Dalai Lama, and thus gain some influence over him in that way? That is one point.' He looked serious. 'There are other possibilities, rather more ominous than that one.'

'Indeed?' said Fenton.

'Indeed. The professor is quite ruthless, I assure you. And I take it his Russian colleagues will not be men of any great sensitivity. For instance, if this Regent were to be – to be removed from the stage, shall we say – then might they not be able to put their own man forward for the job? I could give you more examples of what a completely un-scrupulous man might do, but I had rather not think about them.'

'I think you are exaggerating,' said Fenton. 'Still, my orders are clear. What would you have us do?'

'Whatever Moriarty is planning, he must reach the seat of power in order to carry it through. Is the Regent at this monastery – Ten-gye-ling, is it?' he asked Norbu.

'No, at Lhasa. The various ministries are there, you under-stand,' Norbu explained.

'Then be sure that is where they are heading. And so we too must make for Lhasa,' said Sigerson.

Norbu looked solemn. 'It is already later in the season than I could have wished,' he said. 'We shall have to move fast if we are to reach Lhasa before the winter sets in.'

'That may well be so, but then Moriarty's expedition is facing the same difficulty,' said Sigerson cheerfully. 'Moriarty had to cross Europe, then travel through Russia, and part of China, and that would have to be done as secretly as may be. I believe that he could not have reached the Tibetan border very much sooner than I have done. With luck, we shall get there ahead of them.'

'And do what, exactly?' asked Fenton.

Sigerson raised an eyebrow, for Fenton's tone was that of a man who pours cold water on an overly optimistic suggestion.

Fenton continued, 'I mean to ask, do you have any specific plan in mind? My own orders originally were to observe what may be happening, and if possible to take what steps I might think necessary to counter any hostile incursions into Tibet and the north of India – orders which have been kept deliberately vague purely and simply because we have no real notion of what is going on, and no real standing in those parts. Those orders were then modified to say that I am to obey your orders, and I shall do so, but it might help to know what your plans might be at the very start of our mission. For one thing, despite the fact that Britain may have friends in Tibet, technically we are still outsiders, foreigners forbidden to be there officially. And that must needs constrain what we can accomplish, surely?'

'I understand your concern,' said Sigerson. 'My own concern has been – and necessarily must continue to be – mostly with Moriarty, and perhaps that has led me to overlook the wider issues. Yet if we can frustrate Moriarty's plans, then the rest of it should fall into place as a consequence. I do not see any conflict with your own earlier instructions.'

'I don't know,' said Fenton. 'You seem to be suggesting that the professor is intending to put his knowledge and talents at the disposal of the Russian government, and may perhaps have done so already, in return for – what, exactly?'

'I do not think it too fanciful to imagine that he sees the governor-generalship of India, or some such situation, as his reward,' said Sigerson.

Fenton nodded. 'Just so, that is how I should read it. And by arresting him, or something of the sort, we would effectively prevent that. But the point I am trying to make is that, were the Russians to conclude some sort of treaty with the lamas – though I take Norbu's point as to the political situation, and so forth – or even if they were to seize power by force, to look at it in the most gloomy light, then, even if Moriarty were nowhere to be seen, it would still present a very real danger to British India – after all, I do not imagine there is any shortage of Russian diplomats or generals who might see themselves as ruler of the subcontinent.'

'I quite see that,' said Sigerson. 'And yet I feel you are taking a gloomy view of the prospect ahead of us. Any treaty that Moriarty and his colleagues might conclude with the lamas must needs be secret; it can hardly be with the approval of the Chinese authorities. And if the Regent is an enemy of Russia, there will be difficulties in their way there. I see no reason why we should not conclude our own, secret, treaty if we reach Lhasa first, and can forestall whatever devilry Moriarty has up his sleeve. That must be our main concern, to frustrate his schemes, whatever they may be.'

'And I take it you have the necessary authority to conclude such a treaty, if the Regent is agreeable?' said Fenton. 'For to speak plainly, I do not.'

For a long moment, Sigerson tapped his fingers impatiently on the arm of his chair, and I took that to mean that the answer to Fenton's question was in the negative. Then he smiled, and said, 'If needs be, I can take that authority upon myself.'

Fenton looked at him with a new respect. 'That is good enough for me.'

'Besides,' said Sigerson, 'it may not come to that. If we can but prevent Moriarty and the others reaching Lhasa, if we can do nothing more than preserve the status quo, that in itself may be enough, for the present, at least. Let us not be downcast, gentlemen. Even if Moriarty takes a couple of tricks, we stand a good chance of winning the rubber.' He stood up and stretched. 'And now, gentlemen, if you are quite ready, so am I.'

6

'A journey of a thousand miles begins with but a single step'

Despite Sigerson's eagerness to be off, an eagerness which was, as I have said, shared by Fenton and myself, we decided after a moment's discussion that, as it was by now early afternoon, it would be as well to delay our departure a very little while longer, and leave just before dawn next day. We should then get a decent night's sleep in a proper bed – and there was no telling when we would be able to do that again – and also leave the vicinity of Darjeeling without drawing any unnecessary and unwelcome attention to ourselves.

Fenton had provided Sigerson and me with a native costume of baggy white pantaloons and a long cotton shirt, with an oddly shaped little hat made from some sort of embroidered felt stuff. We changed into these – from thenceforth we should be Indian pilgrims, gone to Tibet for the good of our souls – and Fenton regarded us with an eye as critical as that of any sergeant-major.

'Too obviously new, and far too clean by half,' said he – I may add that the same charge could not honestly be levelled against his own travelling apparel, which would have caused any Savile Row cutter to curl up on the spot. 'Still,' he added, more cheerfully, 'a couple of nights at a Tibetan inn will cure that.'

Fenton had debated for some time as to whether to

attempt to stain the skins of Sigerson and me, the better to disguise us, but had come down against the idea. 'Once you start that,' he explained, 'you must renew the stain every few days, or it looks odd, and there will be difficulties in doing that. You are both pretty sallow, so with that, and the sun, and the lack of proper washing facilities, you should pass muster.'

The phrase about lack of proper washing facilities sounded ominous, but I had endured worse on previous expeditions, so it was with an overall air of cheerfulness that I regarded the immediate future.

Both Fenton and Sigerson, on the other hand, were somewhat subdued. I had no idea what Sigerson might be thinking, for although he had a knack of commanding attention when he spoke, he nevertheless seemed to be one of those men who give little away unless they intend to do so.

Fenton's case was quite different, and when I spoke to him alone during the latter stages of our preparations, he openly expressed some considerable doubt as to Sigerson's entire story.

'I had thought that you were quite convinced,' I protested.

Fenton shrugged. 'It sounded reasonable enough when this fellow was telling it, for he has a very persuasive manner with him,' he said, 'but I was turning it over and over in my mind last night, and every time I thought about it afresh, it seemed the more fantastic. You must remember that I know – or, at any rate, I knew – Professor Moriarty. And I quite liked him, for all his odd little ways – after all, who ever knew a schoolmaster who didn't have some odd little ways? But I don't know anything at all about Mr Sigerson, other than that he is using a false name, and that he has some fanciful tale that my old schoolmaster is now training criminals, for all the world like that old rogue in Dickens – you know the one I mean.'

'Fagin? Yes, it was an odd yarn he spun. But then, he comes highly recommended.'

'Does he?' asked Fenton. 'All we know is that London said they were sending someone, and then this fellow arrives. He claims to have the authority to conclude a treaty with the Tibetan lamas – something that I don't believe the Governor himself could do – and yet he introduced himself with an airy, "Captain Fenton?" and nothing more – no credentials, no letters of introduction – why, not even a visiting card.'

'He could hardly give us his card when he is using an alias,' I felt obliged to say.

Fenton shot me an angry look. 'He could have brought the card of his superior, surely, with a note of introduction? That would have been something. No, Dyce, I confess I am not at all happy about this. And I shall keep a close eye on Mr Sigerson.'

Oho, I thought, I trust we are not setting out in any atmosphere of distrust, for in the wild places it is as well to be able to rely implicitly on one's companions.

For reassurance, I talked to Dass, who regarded the expedition purely as a job of work, but one that would get him away from his family – which seemed an enormous one, by what he said – for a time. 'Not that a man wishes to be parted from his loved ones,' as he told me earnestly, 'but the separation makes the next meeting all the more appreciated.'

Of our little group, only Norbu seemed to regard the adventure as something wholly desirable for its own sake. He made his simple preparations with some sort of religious chant on his lips, and as we set out he remarked sonorously, 'It is said that a journey of a thousand miles begins with but a single step.'

'Do the lamas quote Lao Tze now, then?' asked Fenton.

Very seriously, Norbu said, 'The apparent differences between the religions are made by man. However a man prays, in the high places he may turn his head suddenly and find one of the ancient gods at his side.' And he strode out, his gaze fixed on the distant hills, and in his eyes that curious look of those who love the mountains, a look that neither comrades, nor wife, nor even child, can produce.

The first leg of the journey took us to Gangtok, which is the last town on the Indian side of the border. Gangtok is at no great distance from Darjeeling, a couple of days' brisk walk, and in the event we did walk briskly. Fenton told us that he had toyed with the idea of using mules for this first stage, but decided against it, or rather them.

'Why?' I asked, somewhat irked that I should not be able to ride for part of the way at least.

'Because pilgrims are seldom able to afford mules, and we should have to abandon them in Gangtok in any event,' was Fenton's answer. 'We might get away with it as far as the border, but it would attract attention once we were in Tibet. Moreover, it would only save us – what – a day, at most? Poor compensation for the trouble of looking after them, that, for mules can be awkward beggars.'

And so I had to be content with shanks's pony. By way of mitigating the inconvenience, the air was like wine, and the scenery – as one says on a postcard from Nice – magnificent. Our loads were not heavy, for all our baggage was contained in a leather satchel, or scrip, like those carried by Dan Chaucer's pilgrims. A bowl for our rice, or for that porridge of meal the Tibetans call tsampa, which I would come to know, if not to love, a blanket, and what seemed an inordinately large quantity of that curious green tea of the country, of which more in a moment.

We also carried a generous amount of money, for use in

case of emergency, if anyone needed to be bribed, or the like, but we made sure that it was well hidden about our persons, for, said Fenton yet again, pilgrims were seldom rich men. We carried no weapons, for they would have marked us out as no true Buddhists. I protested about this, for Norbu had said the mountains were full of bandits who would slit your throat for a pair of shabby boots, but Fenton remained adamant, saying that my protest had been noted, but was overruled.

Dass, who was now beginning to enter properly into the spirit of the enterprise, enlivened the journey by inventing a complex pedigree for me. Fenton had assumed that alias of 'Chandra Dass,' that Sigerson had alluded to, a *nom de guerre* he had used often enough before, and was apparently fond of. I was to be Jagdish Dass, cousin to both Ram and Chandra, and something of a rogue, according to my tutor.

Dass went on to invent a wife for me, several children, and a successful business – something in the betel nut line, as I recall – which I had sold in order to wander through the Himalaya seeking enlightenment. This, said Dass, was by no means an uncommon course of action for Indian businessmen, though most of them were somewhat older when they abandoned the world.

'Is not all this just a little too complicated, Dass?' I asked him.

'Not at all, cousin,' said he gravely. 'It is these little details that can easily trip a man up. Now, what were the names of your brothers and sisters, again? And their children's names?'

Thanks to this sort of catechism, by the time we reached Sikkim I had every detail of the history of Jagdish Dass off by heart, and pretty disreputable most of it was, too. That first night we found lodgings at a wayside inn of sorts, and as we sat under the stars with a great throng of merchants and other travellers, Dass took great delight in embarrassing me by constantly referring to a dancer in Hyderabad, to whom I had apparently been attracted for a time, thereby causing my wife to become jealous to the point of violence. Dass had a command of many languages and dialects of which I was ignorant, and he provided many details, which I have no doubt were scurrilous in the extreme, for the further delight of his audience, who could follow what he said. As I could not follow what he said, I was obliged to grin weakly at each new roar of laughter. I suspect that by the end of the evening, most of the others in that inn thought I was slightly feeble minded, though still an object of envy. More to the point, none of them seemed to suspect that I, and the others, were anything other than we appeared to be, and that was some compensation for Dass's slanders.

This inn was quite large, for the road was a well-used one, but Fenton said that there were few inns in Tibet itself. The traveller could ask for a night's lodging at the monasteries, of which there were a great number, in return for a small donation. The only approach to an inn, in the sense in which I understood it, would be found in the larger towns and villages. These inns, added Fenton, were not to be recommended to one's worst enemy.

After three days, we arrived in Gangtok, where we made for the British Residency. The Resident was an old friend of Fenton's, and had evidently conspired in similar schemes before. He asked no questions as to what our business in Tibet might be, but merely issued the permits we needed to cross the border – for the regulations are, as I found out, enforced as strictly by the British as by the Tibetans, indeed more strictly.

We did not stay longer than was necessary to obtain our permits, for it would have looked odd if the Resident had entertained a party of humble Indian pilgrims. And thus, in an hour or so, we were on our way once more. There are no roads worthy of the name in the hills, but there are plenty of tracks worn by the feet of pilgrims and the mules of traders, and we set off from Gangtok along one of these that would lead us to Thimpu, the first settlement of any size across the Tibetan border.

The track led us ever upward, close by the strange and ancient kingdom of Bhutan, which is reputed to be still in the same feudal state as existed in England in the time of the Conqueror. No strangers at all are permitted in Bhutan, save as the personal guests of the ruling family, and these fortunate visitors can, according to Norbu, come and go more or less at will, being provided with food and lodging anywhere in the land. Anyone who does not enjoy this privileged status, however, is simply ignored, and would starve to death if they had not sufficient provisions with them.

Norbu told us all this as we stood on the side of a hill, and gazed down over a valley as green as any in the shires – indeed, I half expected to see the local hunt come galloping round the corner at any moment. I was sorry we had to move on, for I should dearly have loved to take a closer look at that curious land, but both Fenton and Sigerson were champing at the bit.

I may add that there are a very large number of green spots in the hills, a fact which I had only realized fairly recently, and which initially caused me some surprise. Norbu said that we were seeing the place at its kindest, for it was full summer, and that these valleys could be bleak and harsh in the extreme as the year wore on. He added that Tibet itself was much less favoured with green places.

I did wonder if an invading army would necessarily feel constrained to respect the Bhutanese idea of privacy. Norbu smiled grimly, and said that all Bhutanese men are expert archers, reputed to use magic to ensure their arrows never miss. Moreover, any invader must first pass through either Tibet or India, so the country seems safe enough – for the moment, at any rate.

The track now began to lead perceptibly upwards. The last of the greenery was left far behind and below us, and the track was bordered by high rock walls. But, wild as it was, the track was not by any means deserted, for there were great numbers of travellers, in both directions, mostly on foot, but some with mules or yaks, the favoured beasts of burden in those parts.

Many of those we met were pilgrims, as we were supposed to be, or merchants. We travelled for a few miles along with some of the merchants, for banding together, even with strangers one has just met, is a quite common proceeding for greater protection from bandits and the like, an ever-present threat in the mountains, though we encountered none at that time. These merchants had a supply of tea with them, and Norbu insisted upon buying what struck me as an unnecessarily large quantity of the stuff, to add to that which we already carried with us. The drinking of this tea seemed to be Norbu's only weakness, for he was generally undemanding as to his meals.

This tea merits a special mention, for it is an odd drink. It is cured so that the leaf retains its green colour, and I judge that it would be somewhat bitter if drunk alone. It is not drunk alone, though, nor with milk and sugar in the English drawing-room style, nor yet with lemon after the Russian fashion. Instead, it is drunk with salt added, and a generous slab of butter made from yak's milk, as a finishing touch.

The final brew is by no means as unpleasant as it may sound, provided one thinks of it as a soup rather than as a tea. Norbu was exceedingly fond of it, and insisted upon preparing it for us all at every opportunity, saying that as we should be drinking little else in Tibet we might as well get used to it. I thought that I could accustom myself to the taste without too much difficulty, yet I had to hide a smile at the thought of what one of the genteel heroines of the works of Mrs Gaskell might have had to say about it.

7

Into Tibet

Despite the fact that foreigners are notionally forbidden to enter Tibet, there is nothing remotely resembling a frontier post, no guards or officials waiting at the border to check that travellers have the necessary permits. So it was not until we rounded a corner of rock and Norbu pointed to a little village scattered down the side of the hill and said we were now in Tibet, that I realized that we had even passed across the border.

At that time, we were still travelling in the company of those merchants whom I have mentioned, and Norbu had some talk with them regarding permits from the Tibetan authorities to move about the country. The local governor had his dwelling in the village we were now approaching, and he had the power to issue passports.

As might be expected the merchants were already provided with the necessary papers, as they came and went across the border frequently, so all they needed to do was to present their passports to be examined and endorsed, and pay the appropriate taxes.

Norbu thought that we ourselves might have a longer wait, and he went on to make some cutting remarks as to the dilatoriness and insolence of all men in official positions. I thought Sigerson might be offended by this, but he laughed in a good natured fashion, and agreed with everything Norbu said, which caused me to wonder just how official his own standing might be in very truth.

In the event, Norbu's fears were unfounded, for after waiting an hour or so in the courtyard of the governor's house with a large crowd of other applicants, we were summoned before an overworked clerk with a worried expression on his face. We answered a few questions, name, purpose of visit, and the like, and were each issued with a long strip of paper printed in what looked to me like Chinese characters – in return for payment of the appropriate fee, naturally, for although these wild places may be backward in some respects they seldom have much to learn from us in the matter of taxes and imposts.

Once these simple formalities were arranged, we took a quick look round the place and soon found an inn for the night. I might as well describe this inn in some detail here and now, for it was representative of all those we subsequently encountered during our stay in Tibet. That is to say, it was cold, crowded, cheerless, dirty and not entirely free from vermin. There are no beds of even the most sketchy sort, the guest merely curls up on the floor, wrapped in his own cloak or blanket if he is fortunate enough to possess one, or making do with a sort of rough coconut matting, too small to permit him to stretch out at full length upon it, if he has nothing better. The food provided by the innkeepers, where any at all is provided, is best left to the imagination of the reader.

In fairness, the entire country is not well adapted to the needs of the casual traveller, the sightseer, for there are none such, at least as the term is normally used in the west, so it is perhaps invidious to single out the innkeepers for special calumny. And the diet of the ordinary people considered as a whole is very different from what in England would be regarded as wholesome food.

Yet there are plenty of merchants and pilgrims, who surely deserve something better than is currently provided for them. After all, if you are going to bother to run an inn in the first place, it is just as easy – and better for business – to run it in a decent and cleanly fashion. But I am not writing a guide book.

The particular village at which we had arrived – and I regret to say I did not record its name, but from the map I believe it must have been Chumbi – was quite close to the border, and the inhabitants were used to seeing strangers, so we attracted no particular attention, and were able to find a quiet spot and discuss what to do next.

'It would be a pity not to make at least some rough sketches of the country,' I said, 'for they would be of great use in the event of any future expedition coming this way.'

Fenton shook his head. 'That may well be true, but we have already decided that our aim must be to reach Lhasa. Time is no longer on our side, is that not so, Norbu?'

'It is already later in the season than we could have wished,' Norbu confirmed. 'Indeed, it is not by any means certain that we shall reach Lhasa ourselves before the snows begin.'

'In that case,' said Sigerson firmly, 'Lhasa must indeed be our first objective. However,' he added, evidently seeing disappointment on my face, 'there is nothing to prevent our making notes and sketches as we go, if they would be useful later on.'

I kept no regular journal of my time in Tibet, partly because it would have been too dangerous to do so, but mainly because we had very little in the way of paper, and that was needed for such mapping as we managed to complete. And then, although the place had the allure of the forbidden, and there were, indeed, many interesting sights to see, the journey itself – or this early portion of it, at least

– was uneventful, a sure and steady plod upwards and northwards. However, I did make one or two rough notes, which I rendered into a more readable form as soon as I could, and which form part of the basis for this present narrative.

I have said that Dass and I managed to do some mapping. We kept to the main tracks, just as an invading army would be obliged to do, and were thus able to make some sketches and plans which might later prove useful. Neither Fenton nor Sigerson would allow us time to make a proper job of it, though, so we had to work hastily, and mostly from memory, though it was not too difficult to record the main features that would interest a soldier, such as passes where a determined enemy might halt an invading army, and the like.

As supposed seekers after religious truth, we moved freely from one village or monastery to the next, and met with little in the way of official interference. We did not stay long at any one place, though occasionally we were obliged to pay our respects at some particularly revered shrine, and Fenton and Sigerson both fretted terribly at these delays.

We stayed at the monasteries overnight whenever we could, and at the inns when we had no choice, and at every halt Norbu made a point of asking discreetly about the presence of soldiers in the area, the answer being noted down carefully later, and also enquiring whether any strangers had been seen in the vicinity, for we hoped to get on the scent of our antagonists. We did not, however, get any satisfactory answer on this point, which is not really surprising, since we already knew that the Russian party would almost certainly be approaching Lhasa from the northern borders, and so moving in the opposite direction to the line of our own march.

In each town of any size, we always made straight for the house of any man of consequence, and endeavoured to get local approval of our presence. Boldness, said Fenton, was the best course, for if we slunk into the village we should be subjected to all sorts of impertinence, while if we could demonstrate that we were there with the sanction of the local governor or chieftain, we were safe.

Some of these local chiefs, as Norbu had foretold, were a trifle inclined to stand upon their dignity, but most would grant what amounted to a local visa or residence permit in exchange for a few coppers. Some of them, too, were cheerful and cultivated men, who offered us a dry place to stay – in the stables, naturally, not the main house! – and who asked for nothing in exchange but news of the outside world, news which Dass was ever eager to provide, though I fear it was not always entirely accurate.

I saw few signs of what a soldier would recognize as organized military activity. The local governors or chieftains usually had a sort of fortified manor house or castle, called in Tibetan a dzong, as their residence and seat of authority, and these were provided with a band of soldiers to act in some sort of a guard of honour whenever the governor went out collecting taxes and the like. These men struck me as poorly equipped, and few of them showed any sort of enthusiasm for their work, being untidy and having for the most part a sullen appearance, as if they had been compelled to perform a duty which they found distasteful and irksome. As to their drill, I can only say I was glad that none of my friends in the Guards were there to see it.

We were occasionally stopped and questioned on the road, or at the inns, by these soldiers, and once or twice by private citizens, who clearly believed that we were up to no good. However, as we could usually claim that we were in the area with the knowledge and approval of the local dignitaries, our questioners, though they might remain suspicious, were in no position to make life awkward for us.

I was – and still am – at something of a loss to understand why the ordinary people should have this suspicion of strangers. I can appreciate that the occupying Chinese authorities would seek to exclude foreigners, who might undermine yet further their position in Tibet, but the questions usually came from the Tibetans themselves.

Norbu said that it was partly due to the innate suspicion exhibited by all dwellers in remote areas, and partly due to the fact that the Chinese were reputed to have spies and informers everywhere. However, I cannot comment as to how correct this theory may have been.

Whatever the cause, there was suspicion enough. Yet it was not universal, for the ordinary folk frequently invited us into their homes, to share their warmth and their food, though there was little enough of that to begin with.

I attribute this partly to an instinctive sense of hospitality, common enough amongst dwellers in the lonely places of the world, and partly to a desire to acquire merit by showing charity to wandering pilgrims. This business of 'merit' and the acquisition thereof is one of the mainsprings of life in Tibet. Merit can be acquired by hospitality and good deeds, by prayer and meditation, even by rotating the curious prayer wheels which are everywhere to be seen, and which come in all sizes from the portable, for the use of travellers, to the gigantic ones seen at the entrances to the monasteries, which need all a man's strength to move them. Acquisition of sufficient merit is thought to shorten the cycle of death and rebirth, and thus hasten a soul's eventual passage to the Buddhist heaven.

I was touched by the way these simple people shared what little they had, and more than once felt thoroughly ashamed of the deception we were practising on them. I only hope they did indeed acquire that merit which they so richly deserved.

From the border with India to Lhasa does not look any great distance on the map. But the map does not make clear the steepness of the tracks, or their rough condition, nor does it indicate the difficulty in breathing experienced by those who were not born in the mountains. Then, too, we were obliged to make at least some perfunctory show of actually visiting the various monasteries or shrines that formed our excuse for being there in the first place. It would have looked suspicious had we acted otherwise with too great a frequency.

So, our progress was slower than I, for one, had expected. This did not bother me too much, for the novelty of our surroundings was such as to make me want to linger for a closer look. And neither Norbu nor Dass seemed particularly displeased at the speed we made, but both Fenton and Sigerson could have been happier, and, as I say, they both fretted alarmingly at each halt we made, like refined old ladies who are compelled to rush their tea and cucumber sandwiches so that they do not miss their train.

After about two or three weeks, we arrived at the large and prosperous town of Shigatse, and Norbu now began to cast anxious eyes at the sky, to mutter dire warnings about how little time we had left, and to raise the possibility of staying here safe and warm throughout the winter.

'How far are we from Lhasa?' asked Fenton.

'A week, perhaps less,' said Norbu.

'Then let us press on,' Sigerson put in.

Press on we did. And four days later we came to the side of a long valley, and gazed across a broad and rushing river at the rays of the early morning sun reflected from the gilded roofs of Lhasa.

8

Professor Moriarty

Lhasa lies along the length of a low plateau above a river which is, so I understand, a tributary of the great Brahmaputra. We were on the opposite bank to the capital, and had to cross on a ramshackle ferry. As travel in Tibet is only practical in the few months of summer, anyone wanting to visit the capital does not have much time in which to do so, and it looked as if they had all elected to pay their few coppers and cross the river at the same time as we did, for the ferry was doing a roaring trade.

One advantage of the crowds was that we could escape notice that much easier amongst the rest of the throng, the soldiers and guardians at the various palaces being more concerned with keeping the stream of sightseers flowing steadily, rather than with scrutinizing individual faces.

We now had to rely heavily on Norbu's knowledge of the city and its rulers. After a very brief discussion, it was settled that Norbu should meet some of his old friends and colleagues – for it now appeared that he held a high rank among the monks, and in fact possessed a degree approximating to the English Doctor of Divinity, a circumstance which he had hitherto not seen fit to impress us by mentioning – and try to find out whether the enemy had reached the city before us.

After designating a meeting place for later that day,

Norbu went off on his mission, while the rest of us took a walk round the city. Most of the houses are in a low valley between the two hills which mark each end of the town. Each of these hills has a large and imposing building set upon it, the one being the university, and the other the Potala, or Palace of the Dalai Lama. The walls of these are painted in white and red, and the roofs are gilded, so that they are the equal of anything in Venice or Rome. They were impressive enough at first sight to me, who had seen something of the world, so they must be spectacular indeed to the dwellers in the remote villages, who never see a newspaper, much less a picture or a photograph, in all their lives, and who visit the capital for the first time. Norbu had told us that visitors were permitted to look round the Potala, which contained innumerable works of art and the like, but we did not – then, at least – trust our disguises to pass the gaze of the guards who stood before the doors.

Still, even the quite ordinary streets were worth seeing, thronged with soldiers in ceremonial armour of medieval appearance, crowded with merchants selling everything you could think of, and much you would rather not, and, above all, monks and lamas in their hundreds – nay, thousands. The overall impression it made on me was that I had wandered by mistake into the Middle Ages, and every moment I expected one of those old kings, whose dates were thrashed into us at school but which seem curiously elusive when we would recall them now, to come riding round the corner, his knights, squires and varlets at his back.

More prosaically, we took the opportunity to buy some fresh linen, which we now needed rather badly, from one of the merchants, an Indian who had a long and animated conversation with Dass, in the course of which we discovered that our new friend the merchant had not seen or heard anything of any suspicious strangers in Lhasa.

'Although,' as Sigerson remarked as we resumed our stroll, 'that meant nothing, for they would scarcely advertise their presence. They might be here, and in hiding.'

In fact, I was quite enjoying myself, and so was Dass, who gazed at the sights around us as a child gazes at the first snow which it has encountered in its short life. Fenton and Sigerson, as usual, were both trying unsuccessfully to conceal their impatience at this delay, and after trying to cheer them up without any noticeable result, I walked on ahead with the lighthearted Dass, and let them sulk as they would.

At the appointed hour, we hurried back to the spot at which we had arranged to meet Norbu. He was there already, sitting in an angle of the wall, talking to another man, a short, stout man who wore the standard monk's robe, and whose face was wreathed in smiles. As we approached, they rose to greet us.

'This is my cousin, Lobsang Norbu,' said "our" Norbu.

There were smiles, and bows and handshakes all round.

'My cousin has a post in the ministry of the interior,' said Norbu.

'A very humble post,' added the cousin with a broad smile. Like our old friend, he spoke excellent English.

'He knows all about our mission,' said Norbu. 'No,' he added quickly, seeing the look on Fenton's face, 'he is a good friend, I assure you. Also he has his agents throughout Lhasa.'

'And is there any news of our quarry?' asked Sigerson eagerly.

Norbu's cousin nodded his head vigorously. 'A tall, thin, man? His hair arranged in such and such a manner?' He waved his hands over his own head.

'That is Professor Moriarty, no doubt of it!' agreed Sigerson.

'He is here, in the city,' said Norbu's cousin, with another nod of satisfaction.

'Is he, indeed? And doing what, pray?'

'He is lodged in the Potala. He has been petitioning to be engaged in some sort as a tutor to the young Dalai Lama, to instruct him in the ways of the west. As you may know, the current Regent is no friend of Russia, and since the newcomer is obviously an Englishman, the Regent is consequently disposed to be sympathetic to this request.'

'I knew it!' said Sigerson.

'There are, however, many formalities to be gone through first,' Norbu's cousin went on, with a deprecating little smile. 'As a consequence, this professor of yours has been waiting for a week or so for a decision.' He waved a hand apologetically. 'Time does not mean quite the same to us here as it does to you in the west.'

'So he has not actually met the Dalai Lama?' asked Sigerson.

'Not thus far.'

'That is excellent! We have evidently beaten him. Tell me,' said Sigerson, 'can he be arrested, or detained, think you?'

'Oh, yes. If, as you claim, he is intending some harm to the young God-King, then it is positively my duty to arrest him.' Norbu's cousin levered himself to his feet, and waved imperiously towards an angle of the wall. At once, two sturdy young monks armed with heavy staves leapt forward, waiting for instructions.

'If you are quite ready, we can take him now,' said Norbu's cousin. He gave a rapid stream of orders to the two young monks, who took up their positions behind him, then he set off up towards the Potala.

Norbu's cousin had evidently been modest about his official standing, for the guardians at the various gates and doors stood back and bowed politely as he passed. Up several flights of broad stone steps we went, up a couple of wooden ladders, into the very heart of the palace.

In one of the long corridors, lit by a multitude of smoky lamps burning yak's butter, Norbu's cousin paused, and looked about him. 'It is a very old, rambling sort of place,' he told us apologetically, before stopping a passing monk and speaking sharply to him in Tibetan.

The monk scratched his head, then began to answer, but before he had said more than a couple of words, there was a crash and clatter from around a bend in the corridor. Sigerson did not wait for any advice or encouragement, but set off towards the origin of the disturbance as fast as he could. Scenting adventure, I took to my heels after him.

We rounded the angle of the corridor, and almost tripped over a man who lay sprawled out full length upon the floor.

'Give me a hand with him,' said Sigerson, bending to help the man up.

By the time we got the man, another of the monks, to his feet, the others had caught up with us, and Norbu's cousin put a few questions in rapid Tibetan to the monk whom we had just helped up. The man answered him, rubbing his head ruefully as he did so.

Norbu's cousin heard him out, then turned to us with a smile. 'The professor had evidently got wind of what we proposed to do,' said he. 'He has taken to his heels, and I do not think we shall hear from him again.'

'Did he do this, then?' asked Fenton, pointing to the injured man, on whose forehead a great bruise was beginning to be visible.

Norbu's cousin stared down at his embroidered slippers in some confusion. 'One of our countrymen, I fear,' he said at last. 'Perhaps he is just foolish, perhaps he is a rogue – who can say? He has gone with his master, in any event.'

'Well,' said Fenton, 'I think I owe you something of an apology, Mr Sigerson. It seems you were right, and it was Professor Moriarty after all. Still, we seem to have beaten him, and quite easily too.'

Sigerson nodded his acknowledgement of the apology, but then looked grave. 'I have warned you before about underestimating Moriarty,' he said. 'You now know that I comprehended the situation very well, so will you believe me when I say that Moriarty will not be put off quite so easily?'

'I will,' said Fenton at once. 'And yet what is left for him to do? I take it the Regent is well guarded?' he asked Norbu's cousin.

'He is. And after this, the guards will be doubled, and their efforts redoubled.'

'And the lad – that is, the young God-King?' asked Sigerson. 'He, too, is well guarded?'

'You may depend upon it.'

'There you are!' said Fenton triumphantly. 'There is surely nothing to be feared here in Lhasa now? The Potala certainly seems proof against everything but a regiment of artillery, and the Russians would have some difficulty getting one of those here unobserved.'

'There have certainly not been any reports of a large force entering Tibet,' said Norbu's cousin.

'It certainly seems that Lhasa is safe enough,' said Sigerson slowly. 'On the other hand, there is nothing to say that a small, determined force has not entered the country.'

He looked far from satisfied, and he drummed his fingers against a great stone idol that ornamented the corridor. All of a sudden he shot out, 'And the Dalai Lama – until his divinity was recognized, he seemed an ordinary boy?'

Norbu's cousin looked puzzled, but agreed that this was so.

'And his family?' Sigerson went on.

'Ordinary folk, who live in the mountains to the east.'

'They live there still? They have not moved to Lhasa?'

'The boy's mother is here,' said Norbu's cousin. 'She would not be parted from him, though he is now regarded as a God.' He shrugged. 'Who can explain how a woman thinks? It would have been very difficult to prevent her coming.' He sighed, as if at some painful memory. 'But the rest of the family, father and sister, they are still in the village. You understand, it is better that they do not come, better to cut off completely, when such a great change occurs.'

'Quite so,' said Sigerson. 'And the boy presumably feels some affection for his father and sister?'

'Oh, yes. As is quite natural, of course. He is particularly fond of his sister, I believe, for she more or less raised him, the parents having a very harsh life of it, and being busy all day in the fields.'

'Indeed?' Sigerson abruptly ceased his drumming. 'I think it might perhaps be as well if the father and sister were to spend some time in Lhasa.'

'You think they may try to harm them in some way?' asked Fenton, rank disbelief in his voice.

'Not as such. It is more kidnap that I fear, to blackmail or coerce the Dalai Lama into acceding to their demands. If I am wrong, if they are in fact not in any danger, well, then nothing is lost by bringing the boy's family into the capital for a while.' He still looked anxious. 'I only pray we are not too late.' To Norbu's cousin, he said, 'I take it Moriarty will know where the Dalai Lama's family is to be found?'

Norbu's cousin frowned. 'He has been here a few days, so he may have made some enquiries,' said he. 'But he has been carefully watched, and I can swear that he has had no opportunity to get word out of the Potala.'

93

'You are positive?'

'I am. I would answer for it with my life.'

'Well, then,' said Sigerson, 'things are not so bad after all. Perhaps you would furnish us with directions to this village in the east?'

'I will send a man who knows the way,' said Norbu's cousin. 'And you can take these two,' he nodded to the two young monks who had accompanied us from the first. 'A larger party would only slow you down, I think.'

'I think so too,' said Sigerson.

We were quickly provided with a guide who knew the way, and set out at once.

For two days we travelled, under skies of ever deepening greyness, until we came to a tiny hamlet set high in the mountains. The place was silent as the grave, and I think all of us feared the worst. But we knocked on the first door we came to, and a tiny woman, wrinkled and toothless, pointed the way to the cottage we sought.

Norbu hammered at the door, which was opened by a short, wiry man. He looked afraid at first, overawed at seeing all these strangers at his humble home, but spoke readily enough in answer to Norbu's questions, and then summoned his daughter from an inner room. She was about fifteen or sixteen, as far as I could tell, pretty enough but frightened, like her father, at the sight of strangers, and more particularly at the sight of Fenton, Sigerson and me, who were probably the first 'foreign devils' she had ever set eyes on.

Norbu quickly explained that they were summoned to Lhasa, to be with the Dalai Lama, and that satisfied them, for they were simple people, and asked no questions of those in authority over them.

'The thing now,' said Sigerson, 'is whether we should all go back together.'

'Safest not to split our small forces, surely?' said Fenton. 'We do not know how strong the enemy may be.'

'True enough. And yet I should dearly like to take a look at our adversary,' said Sigerson.

Norbu put in, 'Our enemies presumably have never seen the man and girl they seek. If we disguised the girl as a boy, and send these men –' he meant the three monks who were with us – 'back with them, it will look like a father and his four sons. They should not attract attention, even if they are spotted, whereas a larger force might. Moreover, these monks have instructions not to return to Lhasa alive if anything should happen to the God-King's family.'

I may add that these monks were not at all the lean, ascetic men one thinks of as being monks in the west, nor yet the rotund Friar Tuck type of the old legends. They were evidently all farmers' sons, great strapping fellows who must have been part of that surplus male population of which Fenton had told me earlier. I should not have cared to tangle with any one of them in a dark alleyway.

'H'mm,' said Sigerson. 'That may be so, but how would they stand up against rifle fire?'

'How should we?' asked Norbu – for we still had nothing in the way of firearms ourselves. 'A larger party might more easily attract those unwelcome attentions which we are ill-equipped to repel.'

'That is true,' said Sigerson. 'How do the rest of you feel about it?'

'Let us carry on,' I said, 'for I should like to see the enemy.'

'Dass?'

'Why not? The winter will be a long one, so let us have some adventure while we may.'

'Fenton?'

'Oh, I'll go along with the majority. A smaller group may

get back quicker, and not attract attention. Yes, let's take a look at our opponents – perhaps that way I'll finally be convinced that it is the professor.'

We stood watching until the little group was out of our sight, then started off along the track, little more than a footpath, that led out of the village in the opposite direction to that in which we had entered it.

9

Again Professor Moriarty

'There are only two ways into the village,' said Sigerson, as we set out, 'so we must encounter them on this track, for they were not on the other.'

'I still don't see what we can accomplish if we do meet them,' said Fenton. 'We have no weapons, so we can scarcely hope to stop them.'

'Well, for one thing we do not yet know how strong they may be,' said Sigerson. 'That knowledge in itself may be useful.'

'And some weapon may turn up,' added Dass.

Fenton looked unconvinced. 'And the weather seems to be taking a turn for the worse,' he said.

'I confess that does bother me,' said Sigerson. 'However, it will affect our opponents just as much as it affects us. Still, I should not like to be trapped in these high regions without adequate provisions, so let us compromise. We shall travel two days, no more, then set off back for Lhasa, whether we have met the enemy or no, come what may. But if Norbu thinks we should turn back sooner, then we shall. How say you to that?'

We all agreed that this sounded reasonable, and speeded up our pace in order that we might get as far as we might before it was time to return.

All the next day, and the morning after that, we kept up

a good speed under a leaden sky. Fenton, Norbu and Sigerson all seemed to be trying to outdo the others in setting the most gruelling pace that they could. Only Dass and myself, there by accident, almost as a result of our sense of fun, as it were, seemed not to be infected with the sort of silent desperation which spurred the others on. We struggled at the tail end of the little group, giving each other many an ironic look as the man temporarily at the head of the line tackled a yet more difficult gradient.

There were few travellers abroad now, for those who were to spend the winter in Lhasa were already there, while the others had sought their isolated villages or farmsteads, which their summer labours had stocked with food and kindling.

On the morning of the second day, we passed through a tiny hamlet, attracting stares of curiosity from the people, for they knew that all sensible travellers were back at home by now, and Norbu told us that we were approaching the very limit of our outward journey. 'Even if we had not decided to return tomorrow,' said he, 'we should have had to think about starting back to Lhasa if we would be certain of spending the winter in shelter.'

Sigerson looked none too pleased at this, but he evidently meant to honour his promise, for he said nothing, merely nodding to acknowledge that he had understood. Fenton did not trouble to hide his relief, a relief now shared by Dass and me, for the skies were now ominous even to my untutored eyes.

The little hamlet was three or four hours behind us, when we came to a long, low slope that led up into the swirling clouds. Sigerson, at the head of the column, called for a five-minute halt, and we took out pipes or cigarettes.

'It is a pity that we could not devote longer to this part of our journey,' said Sigerson, 'but it cannot be helped.' He looked with some disgruntlement at the cigarette of rank Indian tobacco with which Dass had just presented him. 'Well, Moriarty has presented me with many a three-pipe problem in the past, but – what the devil!'

The last remark was occasioned by the fact that a man had just scrambled over the rim of the rock above us, and now came, half sliding and half running, down the rocky slope towards us. As you may imagine, we looked at him with a good deal of interest. He bore every appearance of being under the influence of some powerful emotion, and as he got nearer we could see that it was fear, for he looked scared to death.

He babbled something in Tibetan, and Norbu translated it for us. 'He says there are bandits, over this hill.'

'That sounds bad,' said Fenton. 'Under other circumstances, I'd have faced them, but as it is –'

'I knew we should have brought some weapons,' I could not resist saying.

Fenton was – very properly – about to put me in my place, when the man said something more to Norbu, in an urgent tone.

'He says, bandits are all dead,' Norbu told us.

'What? How?'

But the man, now somewhat recovered, merely waved to show the way we should go.

'Come along, then,' said Sigerson. 'Dass, you bring this fellow along as quick as you can.'

We set off up the slope, and down the other side. The mist or clouds – the two merge imperceptibly at those heights – prevented our seeing anything until we had gone down the far side for a hundred yards or more, but then we came out to where the atmosphere was clear as crystal, and we halted in our tracks, as if we had all heard an unspoken command.

Scattered over the hillside were the bodies of a score of men, their limbs sprawled out just as they had fallen. I do not think that any of those in our little party could honestly have been described as sensitive, certainly we had all seen death, both peaceful and violent, before. But in those hills, it was such an unexpected sight that it brought us to an involuntary halt, and we stood there a long minute before Sigerson said briskly, 'Let us see what has happened here,' and led the way down the slope.

It was, indeed, fairly obvious what had happened. All the men – poorly dressed, and rough-looking men – had been shot, and simply left where they fell. Sigerson moved from one pathetic corpse to the next; I assumed he was checking to see if any of them were still alive, though it seemed clear enough that it was a forlorn hope.

Sigerson straightened up. 'How would you read this?' he asked.

I shrugged. 'They have been shot. What more is there to say?'

'From the general disposition of the bodies, is it not clear that they were all moving down this slope when they were shot? Furthermore, the absence of any powder marks indicates that they were shot from some distance away.' He picked up one of the rifles that lay scattered all around, and held it to his nose. 'Some of these have not been fired, certainly not recently. That fellow said they were bandits, and – no disrespect to the dead – they certainly look a most villainous bunch, which might suggest that they had been in hiding, possibly higher up in the mist, or behind the rocks scattered about so conveniently for such a purpose, and that they had intended to ambush some group moving along the track which I see at the bottom of the slope here, but in the event they got more than they bargained for.'

'They weren't tailored, either,' said Fenton, who had also

been examining the bodies. 'Most of them have no more than one or two bullets in them, well aimed. Whoever shot these men knew how to make their shots count.'

'Professional soldiers?' said Sigerson, and Fenton nodded agreement.

Norbu said a few words to our informant, whom Dass had now brought to the scene, and listened intently to the gabbled reply.

'He says it was soldiers,' said Norbu. 'Not Tibetans or Chinese, but foreigners. Big men, with beards, and dressed in furs.'

'Cossacks!' said Fenton at once.

'It sounds very much like it,' agreed Sigerson. 'Russians, at any rate, if not the best known specimens of their armed forces. Evidently we have almost come upon the men we seek. Norbu, will you ask how many soldiers this man saw?'

'A hundred, perhaps two hundred,' came the reply. Norbu added on his own initiative, 'but I think that fear may have caused him to exaggerate.'

'Even so, it was a large enough party to cause this slaughter,' said Sigerson. 'And this did not happen very long ago, I would judge. Where did the soldiers go?'

Norbu put the question to our informant, and the reply was immediate, 'Towards the place from which we have come, the home of the Dalai Lama's family, just as we thought.'

'Impossible!' said Fenton. 'The way to the village is the way we have just travelled ourselves. We could not fail to pass them, and we saw nothing.'

Norbu spoke again to our informant, and got a lengthy reply. 'He says there is another way,' Norbu translated. 'A long way round, but the path avoids the second village, the one we saw earlier today.'

'That explains it,' said Sigerson. 'They are avoiding any

settlements, as far as may be, until they are compelled to show themselves.'

Our informant was speaking again, and Norbu, looking elated, said, 'It looks as if we may be able to take a short cut, and head them off without too much difficulty. He says that the way they are taking to avoid the village is a circuitous one, but we can go on foot over the hills.'

Fenton stared at Sigerson. 'Well, do we head them off?'

'It is certainly worth trying, if only to get a look at our enemy, and we may possibly be able to slow them down somewhat, allow our friends more time, even though we may not be able to stop the professor altogether. Norbu, tell our friend here to lead the way.'

Our informant set off across the angle of the slope to our left, and Norbu and Sigerson went after him. But I had noticed that one of the bandits – who had mostly been armed with the sort of home-made weapons that are called 'jezails' in India – had an old but very large and well-cared-for army pattern revolver by his side, and I stooped and picked it up. If we are to tangle with Cossacks, I thought, it might be as well to take some elementary precautions. Evidently Fenton had had the same idea, for I noticed that he too was collecting an armful of weapons from some of the poor fellows who now had no use for them. He saw me looking at him, and gave me a smile, as if we were two naughty schoolboys scrumping for apples, then we set off after the others.

The Tibetan who had told us of the massacre was evidently now fully recovered from the initial jolt of witnessing it, for he set a cracking pace across the slope and then climbed up an almost vertical wall of rock. Only Norbu, who was, presumably, used to this clambering about like a chamois, could keep up with him, the rest of us struggled and gasped some way behind.

Once we had climbed the rock wall, we had a fairly level walk of it, so the going was better, though there was nothing in the way of a track, or even a path, and certainly neither horse nor even mule could have gone that way.

Our guide led us along what seemed to be the top of a high wall of rock, and I was glad that the mist and cloud prevented our seeing exactly how far down it was to the floor of the valley on either side. On we went, now scrambling up more steep slopes, now going down fairly gentle ones, for something approaching two hours.

We were progressing along a narrow path that ran between walls of rock, twelve feet high, on either side. At a bend in the path, our guide halted, waved at us to wait, then moved ahead cautiously. He disappeared from sight for a moment, then returned with a look of excitement on his face, and whispered to Norbu.

'There is a river valley below us,' said Norbu, 'with a little bridge, and we have evidently beaten them to it, for they have not yet arrived at the bridge, but are heading towards it.'

We rounded the bend, and found ourselves on the top of a cliff, which commanded a steep and narrow valley. Just as Norbu had said, there was a little river rushing and tumbling along far below, spanned by one of the makeshift bridges which you see in those parts. There was a track of sorts on either side of the river, and on our side, but still half a mile off, a file of mounted men were riding towards both us and the little bridge. There were certainly not a hundred riders, but it was a large group, a couple of dozen men, and they all looked competent and well-armed.

'Cossacks, or I'm a Dutchman,' muttered Fenton.

Sigerson had gone ahead, and was examining the edge of the cliff, a look of vexation clouding his brow. 'The rock is rotten just along here,' said he. 'With a half pound of powder we might have brought the whole lot down, prevented their crossing the river here, and given ourselves an extra day.' The annoyance he felt was written plainly upon his face.

Fenton gave a little cough, as if deprecating his foresight. 'I took the liberty of helping myself,' he said, holding up the equipment he had collected earlier. 'Those poor chaps didn't look as if they'd be needing it, but I thought that we might find it useful if we had to face the Imperial Russian Army. There is plenty of powder here.'

'Well done,' said Sigerson. 'Now, if we work quickly, for I would not wish to harm them if it might be avoided –'

He and Fenton packed a large quantity of the black powder into cracks in the cliff edge. It took some time to do it properly, and the leading riders were all but at the bridge as they finished.

Fenton gazed down, and frowned. 'We have left it a bit late.'

'No matter,' said Sigerson firmly. 'They are soldiers, and know the risks they take. Light the fuses!'

Fenton did as he was bid, and we set off hastily back the way we had come, rounding the bend in the track as there was an explosion, which deafened us for a moment, amplified as it was by the surrounding walls of rock.

'That should do it,' said Sigerson with some satisfaction.

Fenton, who had been in the rear, said, 'I think the leading riders were caught in the fall, and had no time to pull back.'

'Ah, that's a pity,' said Sigerson with no sign of emotion. 'I wish it might have been avoided, but there it is. Well, Captain Fenton, I think you have achieved what you were ordered to do, to assess the situation and prevent the enemy from doing any harm to our interests. Our best course now seems to be to return to Lhasa, to determine whether we can make any diplomatic progress. The leaders were lost, you think?'

'I'm certain of it. So that means that the professor – if he was with them, which is still not proven – can be no further danger to us.'

'It would indeed be comforting to think so,' said Sigerson with a smile as enigmatic as that of the Mona Lisa.

10

'A most interesting man'

For two days we went back the way we had come. It is safe to say that each one of us felt pretty well satisfied with ourselves, and each showed it in his own way.

Fenton and I were content that we had halted the enemy's march in so soldierly a fashion. Dass was, I think, still fascinated by the explosion, which had, I must admit, been quite spectacular, and expressed his satisfaction that the job had been done cleanly and with some concrete result, 'For,' said he, 'in this line of work there are sometimes a good many loose ends.' Norbu sympathized with the riders who had perished, but recognized that it had been necessary in order to help his countrymen. Sigerson too was pleased enough when I asked him, though he still gave some pretty broad hints that we had not heard the last of our enemy, a proposition which Fenton took leave to doubt – to me, and in private, at any rate.

After two days, we passed through the last village before Lhasa, and came to another deep valley, through which rushed a fairly broad river – I think it was the same branch of the Tsangpo which borders Lhasa, but it may have been merely a tributary stream, for there are many little rivers in the mountains.

The narrow track led steeply downwards to a ramshackle bridge, not so very different from the one at which we had blocked the enemy's advance, and we set off down it. We had got about halfway down the side of the cliff face, when suddenly a shot rang out from the wall of rock high above us.

Instinctively we threw ourselves down at full length, sought what little shelter there was, and cowered there.

Scarcely had we done this, when there was a second shot, and by this time I had recovered my composure sufficiently that I could make out that it was someone higher up on the track along which we had just walked who was doing the shooting. It must, therefore, have been someone who had followed us, waiting to get to a position of vantage. He had succeeded, for we were as helpless as fish in a barrel where we were. We lay there in silence, waiting for yet another shot, but none came.

Five minutes, long minutes, passed, then ten.

'Dyce, can you see anyone up there?' asked Fenton, at my side.

I looked cautiously up, but could see nothing. 'All clear as far as I can make out.'

'If there were anyone up there, why should he wait, when we are so completely at his mercy?' wondered Fenton. 'Have you your pistol?'

'Yes.'

'Then be ready if he shows himself.'

Before I could speak, Fenton had left his hiding place. He edged his way back the way we had come, and the rest of us watched, fully expecting the worst. I still had the ancient revolver and a dozen cartridges, and I had more or less marked the spot where our assailant had been, so I hoped that if he tried again I might be able to get off one or two shots that would count, but everything was quiet.

Fenton reached the top of the cliff, and he carefully raised his head, and looked back the way we had come, before shouting down to us, 'There's nobody here now.'

He scrambled down to rejoin us. 'Evidently we did not succeed in disposing of them completely,' he remarked drily.

'I had expected something of the sort,' said Sigerson. He glanced around. 'But what ails Norbu?'

We looked where he pointed. Norbu, who had been at the head of our little procession, still lay where he had thrown himself. Sigerson hastened over to him, then stepped back with an oath.

'The second shot did not miss,' said he.

The rest of us hurried over, but there was now nothing anyone could do. The second shot had gone through Norbu's heart.

There was no point stopping to mourn him here. We improvised a kind of stretcher with our cloaks and blankets, and started off once more, intending to take Norbu's body to his cousin in Lhasa.

'I blame myself for this,' said Sigerson bitterly as we went.

'You should not,' Dass told him. 'Norbu was every bit as much a soldier as those unfortunate Russians, and he knew the risks just as well as they did.'

'No,' said Sigerson with a curt shake of his head. 'Were it that and nothing more, I should think the same as you. But poor Norbu was in the lead when he was shot, and he was of much the same size and appearance as I am. They intended to kill me, not him, and that is what I mean when I say I am responsible.'

We crossed the bridge, and set off up the path on the opposite side, the path that would lead us to Lhasa.

As we reached the top, our way was blocked by a very tall man, wrapped in furs. He did not venture any sort of greeting, nor did he move aside as we neared him, and I wondered what on earth he thought he was doing, for he could see that we had a heavy burden. It was impossible for us to pass him on the steep and narrow track, struggling as we were with poor Norbu's body, and it was a long way down to the valley below us.

Sigerson turned round, and motioned to us to set Norbu down by the path side, then he walked up to the man who stood there.

'Good evening, Professor. I had expected you.'

'Good evening, H——,' said the man in English. The blank does not signify an oath that I wish to conceal in some prissy Jane Austen fashion, but a name, and the name was not "Sigerson". It was unknown to me – then, at least, though it has become somewhat more familiar to me since, for its owner is famous the world over.

'My name is "Sigerson" in these parts, a shift which I am sure you will respect. Well, Professor, I take it that you have come to finish the business we left half done at Reichenbach?'

'Just so – Sigerson.' He gazed about him, with a curious oscillating motion of his head. 'The surroundings are uncannily similar, are they not?'

'Indeed. But this time I have the companions.'

'Come, come, Sigerson!' said the professor with a laugh. 'You would not stand upon ceremony, I feel sure. I am, by the way, very sorry that your friend should have come to such a sad end,' he waved at Norbu's body. 'I told Igorov that you were not so easy to kill, but he quite insisted.'

'He is not with you, then, this – Igorov?'

'We parted company, I fear. He is a brilliant man in his own way, but somewhat headstrong. He would insist upon trying to dispose of you once and for all, after you spoiled his plans in that precipitate manner – I assume that the explosion and landslide was your work, of course? Yes? I had thought as much. And now he has set off for home, I have no doubt, probably in some dudgeon after the failure of his main mission, but with the quite illusory compensation of having encompassed your death. I, on the other hand, wished to make absolutely sure. So I am alone, and at your disposal. I am also unarmed,' he added, staring at the revolver in my hand, 'so you will please tell your friends, who look young enough to be quite impetuous, not to interfere.'

'You will do as the professor says,' Sigerson told us. He walked forward a little way towards the professor, who was removing his travelling coat.

'But surely, gentlemen' protested Fenton, 'you do not propose to brawl like a couple of navvies on pay day? Apart from the obvious dangers of doing so in so wild a spot, it seems impious with poor Norbu lying here. You, Mr Sigerson, I have grown to know and respect you – and you, professor! Why, I was one of your pupils, ten years or so ago. Do you not recognize me?'

The professor stared at him. 'One impudent puppy is much like another,' he said in an offhand way.

Fenton, looking abashed, and more than a little offended, relapsed into silence.

Sigerson was now standing on the very edge of the path, with a sheer drop at the side of him. 'Mind, now,' he told us, 'you are not to interfere in any way. If by some chance I should not be here at the end of our little contest to advise you, then I leave it to you to decide what is to be done with the professor here.'

The professor bowed to him in an ironic fashion, then – before I had worked out what they proposed to do – he made a clumsy rush towards Sigerson, for all the world as if he intended that they should both go over the edge of the path and plunge into the river far below.

Although they were much of a size, Sigerson was in the

prime of his life, and was in good training – he had, for example, frequently set the pace for the rest of us on the route to Lhasa. By contrast this professor was about sixty, as near as I could judge, and his leanness was not that of an athlete, but that of some old, dried-out, leathery don, fit only for shuffling round his library.

Sigerson met his shambling onslaught, and they wrestled for a short moment, before the professor stumbled on the edge of the path, let out a hideous scream, and clutched frantically – and hopelessly – at the air, as he toppled slowly but surely backwards, looking like the figures one sees in a nightmare, where the most ordinary action seems to take years.

Sigerson, a look of horror on his face such as I have never seen before or since, leapt desperately towards him, his arms outstretched as if he would catch him, but it was too late. The scream did not end until the professor hit the water far below.

It all happened so quickly that the rest of us had not been able to move from where we stood. As the professor went over the edge, Sigerson slumped down on the very lip of the path, like a rag doll, and that galvanized us into action.

Fenton and I took one look over the edge, but it was evident – and had been from the dreadful, abrupt, way that the scream had been cut off – that nothing could be done for the professor, so we turned our attention to Sigerson.

Between us, we lifted him up. He was unhurt, there was not a mark on him, but his face was a ghastly white, and there was a haunted look in his eyes.

He stared at me. 'How many more times?' he asked, and then I think he must have fainted, for he went limp in our arms.

We scurried round, trying to revive him. Dass donated a

small and secret hoard of brandy for the purpose, and eventually Sigerson groaned, and stared up at us. But his eyes were now blank, without a sign of any human emotion in them.

'He has had a dreadful jolt,' said Fenton – although indeed that much was obvious. 'We had best get him back to the capital, and try to find a doctor of sorts.'

Fenton and I carried Norbu, while Dass followed behind, leading Sigerson by the hand with the innocence of a child leading a blind man. And thus we entered Lhasa, to the curious stares of the crowds who turned out to see five men, three live, one dead, and one who walked as if in a dream.

We explained to the curious sightseers that we had been attacked by bandits, which was near enough to the truth, and found an inn with an empty room.

Dass went off to find Norbu's cousin, who brought two or three of his fellow monks along, sturdy, silent men who took over the necessary arrangements. Norbu's cousin already knew something of our mission, so we told him the truth.

'My cousin told me of the dangers,' said he calmly enough. 'He was willing to accept them, and had no fear of dying – as you know, we believe that we shall be reborn again and again until we are free from the wheel, and become one with the infinite – so you need shed no tears for him. But now, what of our other friend here?'

Sigerson did, indeed, demand some careful attention. The glazed look which had been in his eyes since the professor's death had gone, and he seemed to have developed some sort of brain fever, for he lay on the makeshift bed, tossing from side to side like a man who had a bad dose of malaria, and muttering and mumbling to himself.

Norbu's cousin ordered him moved to a room within the Potala, and we were also provided with clean, albeit Spartan, accommodation within the same building. Perhaps I ought to digress here for a moment to explain that the Potala is not a single palace as the word is used in Europe, but a congeries of buildings of every shape and size, all lumped together over the hill on which it stands. Some of the lower levels correspond to what in London would be the offices of the various government departments, and house the various ministers – all of them lamas – and their staffs.

The local doctors took charge of Sigerson, treating him with a mixture of herbal decoctions and magic chants, while Fenton, Dass and I took turns sitting by his side through the night.

By way of some small consolation, we learned from Norbu's cousin that the Dalai Lama's father and sister had reached Lhasa without any untoward incident, and it was good to have this confirmed, though we had assumed it would be so, once we had halted the Russians in so spectacular a fashion.

For two weeks Sigerson hovered on the very brink of insanity, apparently not knowing where or who he was, and unable to recognize anyone around him, so that we wondered if it had been worth it after all, or whether the price had been too high. 'He, too, was a soldier, and knew the risks,' muttered Fenton, when I put it to him in those terms. But for all that, I noticed that he was seldom long away from Sigerson's bedside.

One night when it was my turn on duty and I was alone in the sickroom, I remember that Sigerson opened his eyes and stared at me as if he knew me, and I thought that it was over, and that he was cured, but he slapped me on the back, and called me, 'Good old W——!' over and again, and talked quite lucidly, as it seemed, of the many and varied adventures which we had been through together. It was not until much later that I managed to work out who the mysterious W—— really was.

From what he said in these delirious ramblings, it was pretty clear that "Sigerson", as I shall continue to call him, had been through a great deal – far more, I am certain, than most men could cope with and retain their sanity – in the few months immediately prior to our meeting him. He spoke of numerous attempts on his life, of a web of evil and corruption spread over the entire length and breadth of England – nay, Europe – a web which had Professor Moriarty at the centre of it. If the half of what Sigerson said in his ravings was true, then the professor had indeed been the most double-dyed villain in the whole history of crime.

And Sigerson kept coming back again and again to some nightmarish scene on the edge of a cliff. This was fairly obviously a reference to the death of Professor Moriarty, but it seemed to have become an obsession with him, a hideous recurring nightmare, for he spoke as if it had happened more than once.

Then, quite abruptly, the fever broke, and Sigerson was himself again. Or almost himself, for there was still a haunted look in his eyes. Moreover I am certain that the nightmare was still with him, because for a long time after that his sleep was troubled, and he woke at least once each night, drenched with sweat, and with a look on his face that frightened anyone who saw it.

The onset of winter meant that we should be confined to Lhasa for several months, and now that Sigerson was up and about once more, if not exactly his old cheerful self, we could concentrate on the second stage of our mission, and attempt some sort of diplomatic overtures to the Tibetan authorities, though these negotiations were necessarily conducted in strict secrecy.

Norbu's cousin had told us that he had some small office in one of the ministries, but it was clear that he had been modest. From what Norbu had said about his cousin's having spies throughout Lhasa, or something of the sort, I concluded that the cousin had some high office in the secret service, or its Tibetan equivalent, though naturally we did not deem it politic to inquire into his exact standing. I do know that he must certainly have had some influence to get us rooms in the Potala in the first place, and he was always treated with great deference by those monks who accompanied him.

Since Norbu had told his cousin why we were there, and the cousin had not had us arrested, we concluded that the cousin was as sympathetic to the British cause as our old friend had been, and told him the whole story accordingly. Just as we had hoped, he nodded when we had done, and said, 'I had promised my cousin to arrange what I could. If you wish to proceed, I can introduce you to many of the chief lamas, and we should be able to achieve something. However, only the Regent himself can say the final word, and it will take time to arrange a meeting with him. He is watched by the agents of the Chinese overlords, who are suspicious of any dealings with foreigners. Also many of our own people are unsympathetic to Britain. But I shall do what I can.'

He was as good as his word, and there ensued a succession of meetings, usually held in the evening, with a succession of mysterious figures in red and gold robes. I myself was excluded from most of these, as being too young and inexperienced, but Fenton gave me a summary of what had taken place, from which I gathered that our party was making slow but steady progress.

Sigerson, too, seemed quite pleased with the way things were going. According to Fenton, it was Sigerson who took the lead in most of the talks, for he seemed to possess a natural flair for diplomacy.

Sigerson had now fully recovered his senses, though the haunted look never left him. He took us aside the first or second day after he was on his feet, and said, 'Gentlemen, the professor inadvertently revealed my true name. I do not know whether it is familiar to you, but I should like you to try to forget it, along with anything I might have let slip in the course of my recent indisposition.' We solemnly promised, and as you see I have kept my promise here. Sigerson seemed somewhat reassured by our undertaking, but as I say the haunted look, and the nightmares, persisted.

After a month or six weeks of these secret talks, Fenton came to me one day in great glee, and said that Norbu's cousin had now arranged matters so that they might meet the Regent, to gain final approval for the secret treaty that would mean that Britain could enter Tibet when the Chinese Empire finally collapsed. Once again, I was to be excluded, though I might go along and wait outside.

On the appointed evening, Norbu's cousin solemnly and silently conducted us into the Red Palace, the true heart of the Potala, a giant treasure house on some thirteen or fourteen floors, the floors being linked by innumerable ladders. I was conducted into an antechamber, where a couple of large, silent, young monks motioned me to sit down and wait, while Fenton and Sigerson were led off down a corridor lined with gigantic statues of demons, made from gold and silver.

I tried vainly to interest my companions in some idle conversation, but soon wearied of it, and settled down to try that meditation that was universally practised there. I am delighted to say that I succeeded to such an extent that I fell asleep, to be woken with a start a couple of hours later by Fenton.

'Come on, you lazy young cur,' he said cheerfully.

'And Sigerson?' said I, looking round.

'Oh, he has a special interview on his own.'

'Oh?'

Fenton was silent, but full of a sort of suppressed gleeful-ness, until we had reached our own quarters, then he ex-plained that the interview had gone very well. The Regent had – wisely, I feel sure – refused to commit anything to writing, but had assured them that a British force would meet with little or no opposition from the Tibetan forces. Fenton and Sigerson had risen to take their leave, but the Regent – 'A queer old bird, with a look of possessing the wisdom of the ages about him,' at least according to Fenton – had spoken to Norbu's cousin, who was acting as inter-preter, and Sigerson was bidden to remain. 'Though what he wants, I can't say,' added Fenton.

In the event, Sigerson did not reappear for three days. Then he strolled in as if nothing out of the ordinary had happened, and I saw at once that the haunted look was gone from his eyes, and he was truly himself once more.

'Well, gentlemen,' was all he said, 'I am quite at your disposal now.'

Naturally we asked what had happened, but he only shook his head, and gave us that enigmatic smile.

'But the Regent,' demanded Fenton. 'What think you of him?'

Sigerson smiled again. 'An interesting man,' said he. 'A most interesting man.'

11

Westward Ho!

Even if I could remember all the minutiae of our daily existence, I would not wish to give any detailed blow-by-blow account of how we passed the winter of 1891, and the early part of 1892, in Tibet, for the reader would find it wearisome.

It is true that everything in our new surroundings was strange, even exotic, and that there was much to do and much to learn. We found no difficulty about moving about the capital, and were even admitted without any questions as students in the schools of theology and medicine, though I regret to say that none of us, with the possible exception of Sigerson, were very apt pupils. Still, it was fascinating to watch the other students committing the sacred texts to memory, for such is the royal route to academic success in the Tibetan colleges. And the debates, vigorously conducted, were always a source of entertainment as well – I have no doubt – as instruction.

Despite that, though, the enforced idleness soon began to pall. Dass and Sigerson, both of whom possessed some private Stoic philosophy, coped best with the enforced seclusion from the outside world, but eventually they, too, caught that ennui which had affected Fenton and me almost from the start, and it was with considerable relief that we hailed the spring thaw, and could at last start to make our preparations for the return to India.

We had made a good many friends among the monks and lamas, and although I cannot truthfully claim that a large crowd turned out to wave us off, still there were a good many handshakes and kind words before we left.

As it was spring, and the snow was starting to melt, the journey back to Darjeeling was easier with each day that passed, with the result that three uneventful weeks after setting off from Lhasa we arrived back in Darjeeling, and made our way to Fenton's bungalow.

By the time we had bathed and shaved and generally made ourselves respectable – a process which I may say took some considerable time – it was getting too late to think of contacting Fenton's superior and making our report in person. Fenton accordingly sent a message to say that we were back, and would be giving a full account of ourselves on the following day. And then we sought our beds, the first time in something over a year that we had not been obliged to curl up on an earth floor, or amongst a pile of hay. I do not know how the others fared, but I can say that in my own case the novelty meant that I could not get off to sleep for some considerable time, but then I knew nothing until ten or eleven the next morning, when Fenton quite literally turned me out of my bed onto the hard floor.

At breakfast, which was somewhat later than would be regarded as respectable, Fenton received an answer to his message, which said that his chief would be busy all day, but could see us in the evening.

'Fairly typical, in this line of work,' was Fenton's laconic comment. 'The colonel probably has a dozen different ploys in hand at the moment, and, since we have returned safely, he will have gathered that we have been successful.'

I thought this over for a moment, then, 'You mean that had we not been successful, your chief would not have expected us to return? Death or glory, that sort of thing?' I asked.

Fenton nodded. 'I did not say as much at the outset, for it might have put you off,' he remarked.

'Well –' I began, but Sigerson laughingly intervened.

We now bade farewell for the time being to Dass, who wanted to be off to see his family. Then, since we could do nothing until later, we tried to catch up with events in the wider world.

Fenton was a member of the Darjeeling Club, and the secretary made no difficulty about Sigerson and myself being admitted temporarily, so we were able to talk with the local army and Indian Civil Service officers about what had occurred during our absence.

There was a library of sorts at the club, and Sigerson immersed himself in the piles of back numbers of the London papers. I could not help noticing that he seemed particularly amused by a fairly recent issue of the *Strand*, a circumstance which intrigued me greatly. When I looked over the list of contents myself later that afternoon I could see little that seemed likely to be of interest, with the possible exception of a detective yarn by a man called Doyle, which I had no time just then to read. I may add that when I was later able to do so, it explained almost everything about the history of 'Sigerson', and also much about what he had said when he was raving with fever in Lhasa.

The look of amusement vanished, though, when Sigerson found an old copy of *The Times*. He read it with an expression of irritation, and threw the paper down with an exclamation of disgust.

'Bad news?' I felt compelled to ask.

'No more than I expected. I see from the law court reports of a year ago that a couple of the villains who were

Moriarty's chief lieutenants managed to walk free after the jury refused to accept evidence which quite plainly implicated them in crimes of the foulest nature. Still, I am certain that they are constitutionally incapable of living lives of blameless purity, so no doubt there will be other opportunities for justice to take its proper course.' He retrieved and tidied up the newspaper, replaced it among its fellows, and laughed. 'On balance, I think it is better this way, for Moriarty was well worth a pair of these lesser villains. And now, if we can find Fenton, I think we might sample the wine of the country.'

We took a walk round the town, and after taking some refreshment in one of the many little teashops in the place – Darjeeling tea, naturally – it was time to call upon Fenton's superior, a Colonel Munro Stark, whom I had not hitherto met.

Colonel Stark was another of those men – dark, small, nondescript – who, like Fenton, could pass for a native, if he had been clad in a tattered robe instead of the dress uniform he had put on ready for some reception or another later that evening.

'You have done well indeed,' he said to Fenton and me when we told him of our journey and our negotiations with the Tibetans. 'Be sure it will not go unremarked by the powers that be. I wish I had been there with you, for you seem to have had an exciting time of it. A pity that much of what happened cannot be generally divulged, for it would make interesting reading.'

Fenton flushed. 'I had thought that perhaps some account of our expedition might not come amiss, sir,' said he. 'The part played by Dyce and myself must, of course, be suppressed, as must the Russian involvement, but I confess that I could see no very great objections to reporting some of the less controversial adventures of Mr Sigerson of

Norway, unless either of you see fit to forbid it?'

'Not I,' said Sigerson.

'Nor I, provided that I can read and approve the final draft,' said Colonel Stark.

I may add that, although I subsequently twitted Fenton unmercifully about his unsuspected literary leanings, he did make an excellent job of the finished descriptive articles, which received wide circulation and attracted a good deal of interest in learned circles.

'And you, sir,' the colonel went on to Sigerson, 'you have, I understand, accomplished the task you were set by London?'

Sigerson nodded. 'I have. And moreover I have accomplished the more difficult task I had privately set myself.'

Colonel Stark raised an eyebrow, and when Sigerson did not elaborate, he said, 'You have evidently had a most interesting time of it, and must tell me as many details as time will allow.' He took out his watch, and added, 'We have two hours or so before I must leave, so pray begin your account.'

Fenton accordingly did so. When he mentioned the name Prince Igorov, which Professor Moriarty had used, Stark's brow clouded.

'Is the name known to you, sir?' asked Fenton.

'No. Or, that is to say –' Colonel Stark broke off, and went across to his desk, where he unlocked a drawer and rummaged among some papers. 'Ah, yes, here we are.' He brought a large sheet of blue paper across to us. 'I knew I had seen the name recently, and here he is. Prince Alexei Ilyich Igorov, that the fellow? Very possibly an alias, mind you.'

Sigerson remarked, 'It sounds a bit like the central character in an unfinished opera by the late Russian composer, Monsieur Borodin.'

'Does it, indeed? Then very possibly that is where he got the name from,' said the colonel. 'Well, anyway, his name – Igorov, not Borodin – appears on his report from one of my agents in Teheran. The prince has apparently turned up there, at the Russian Legation.'

'The devil he has!' exclaimed Sigerson. 'And what can he be doing in Persia, I wonder?'

Fenton and Colonel Stark laughed out loud, while Sigerson and I stared from one to the other of them in some astonishment.

'Your pardon, gentlemen,' said Colonel Stark. 'You could, perhaps, scarcely be expected to know what strikes us as so amusing. However, the presence of a Russian agent – another Russian agent, I may say – in Persia is easily explained, when you think about it.' He walked over to a large coloured map which hung upon the wall. 'Here,' said he, tapping the map with a long ebony ruler, 'is Russia. Plenty of coastline, you observe, but look where it all is. Here, the Baltic, and there, Vladivostok, plenty of seaports, but all of them ports which are blocked solid by ice every winter. More than anything, Russia desires – needs – a warm water port. That is one of the main reasons for the Russian desire to acquire India, or at the very least a toehold in India. We – by which I mean the British – have reasonably good relations with the Persians, but the Russians never cease trying to extend their own influence there.'

Sigerson frowned. 'You make it sound as if it were a continuous process, Colonel.'

'M'mm, it is. A posting to the Legation there – British or Russian – is generally regarded as a cosy billet, precisely because the political situation is static, not to say stagnant. The Shah's regime is benevolent enough, corrupt in parts, of course, as all those fellows are –' (I need not add that the Colonel was one of the old school, particularly in his approach to what he would undoubtedly call 'natives') – 'but Nasr ed-Din is enlightened enough to look to the west for guidance. A useful buffer for British India, as some politician remarked. And likely to remain that way, unless and until there is some violent upheaval.'

'Thank you, Colonel,' said Sigerson, 'that gives me an admirable thumbnail sketch of the place. But the point I was making is that, given that there are already career diplomats on both sides trying to advance the interests of their several countries, and given that even they would appear from what you say to have little chance of changing things, then why on earth should the Russian government bother to send this Prince Igorov there into the bargain?'

'I see what you mean,' said Colonel Stark thoughtfully. 'Perhaps they hope that he will ginger things up a bit? London does that sometimes, sends someone out here to stir us up, and the Russians probably do the same. Probably shouldn't say that to you, seeing that you were sent here to stir us up,' added the bluff old soldier.

Sigerson laughed. 'Hardly that, Colonel. Nor would I presume to do anything of the sort. No, my mission was a very specific one, for which I happened, by force of circumstance, to be better qualified than anyone here. Well, no doubt you have the right explanation.'

'Forgive me, sir,' said Fenton, 'but it may be that the prince is acting on his own initiative, that he has some sort of roving commission from the Tsar, and that he has spotted something he might turn to his advantage – or to Russia's advantage, that is to say.'

'Now that is very likely,' said the colonel. 'And, of course, he might easily do both – go along to see what mischief he can make on his own account, and at the same time put the fear of God into the idle beggars at the Legation. Yes, that would make sense. Well, nothing we can do about him now,

I'm afraid, now that he's out of our territory, so I'll pass the word on to Teheran to keep a close watch on him.' He sighed. 'Pity that the situation in Afghanistan looks so acute just at the moment, or I'd have asked you to go into Persia, Captain Fenton.'

It sounded the sort of adventure that every young man dreams about: travel, excitement, danger, and the prospect of glory and advancement at the end of it all. I should dearly have loved to volunteer to undertake the task of pursuing this mysterious Russian prince myself, but the sight of the colonel in his finery prevented my speaking.

Sigerson asked, 'But surely the British Legation have their own men there?'

Colonel Stark shook his head. 'Only in a very limited way. Oh, they keep watch on the other embassies or legations, bribe the doormen and what have you, send a note of anyone out of the ordinary, like this Igorov. But things really are so settled there just at present that there is no-one who might do anything more – adventurous, shall we say? No reliable agents who could be entrusted with the task of following the man, see what exactly he is up to, if he should leave the capital.' He rubbed his chin as if deep in thought, and looked hard at Sigerson. 'I don't suppose –'

'Hardly, Colonel!' Sigerson laughed. 'My task here is done, and I now look to return to London as soon as may be. And I scarcely think myself fitted for what you have in mind, for I am neither a diplomat nor a cloak-and-dagger agent. Why, I don't even speak Arabic.'

'I do, sir,' I blurted out – for I could keep silent no longer.

'You, Dyce?' said the colonel.

'Yes, sir. It has been useful to me more than once, in the course of mapping and surveying. My superior officers will assure you that I am quite fluent,' I added.

'I am sure they will.'

'Moreover,' I went on, keen to make out my case, 'I can even manage a few hundred words of Farsi, which is the Persian variant, and somewhat different from what one might call the classical Arabic. And then if you, Mr Sigerson, are quite set on returning to London, why, Persia is not so very far from the direct route in any event. You would have to go via Colombo and Egypt, would you not? Well, Persia is only a short distance out of your way.'

I had half expected the colonel to utter some sharp rebuke for my presumption, but he was not that sort of man. Instead, he asked Sigerson, 'Come now, sir, what say you? As Dyce says, it would not be too great a detour, nor too great a hardship. And the government would pay your expenses, on a reasonable scale, of course. Well?'

Sigerson laughed heartily. 'Well, indeed! I have the distinct impression that I am the victim of some cunning fraud, designed to make me do that which I would not, like some provincial businessman who comes to London to be rooked by our native tricksters.' He looked at me, his face serious now. 'Lieutenant Dyce, do you think your abilities are equal to the task of countering the endeavours of a determined agent of the Russian government?'

'I should like to think that they are, sir, though only time will tell whether I flatter myself.' Boastful, I allow, but what man at twenty-odd would say otherwise?

'And are you prepared to put yourself under my orders?' asked Sigerson.

'If Colonel Stark instructs me to do so, sir.'

'Colonel?'

'If you, Mr Sigerson, are prepared to act for us in this matter, then I think you may count on our assistance in every possible way.'

'In that case,' said Sigerson, 'I suppose I had better say yes.'

The colonel looked pleased. 'I hoped you would say as much. Now, the overland routes would take too long, and they all lead through dangerous regions, so you had best go by sea. There are regular sailings to Aden, and from there you can get some smaller vessel to one of the Gulf ports. You will have to make you own way overland, I fear, but that should not be too difficult at this time of year. Let us hope he has not moved on before you get there.'

'And if he has done so?' asked Sigerson.

The colonel looked at me, a wicked expression in his eyes. 'Well, Dyce? If he has moved on, what would your course of action be?'

'To pursue him, sir, until we ran him to earth.'

'Good man! Does that satisfy you, Mr Sigerson?'

Sigerson laughed. 'It is the response I would expect from a soldier and a man of action, Colonel. Well, we shall see what may be done. It is a good cause, after all.'

Once the matter had been settled in this way – a most satisfactory way from my point of view – our preparations were quickly made, with the result that two days later Sigerson and I found ourselves aboard a steamer bound for Aden.

12

Igorov

I do not know what the state of things may be these days, but certainly at the time of which I write communications from Aden along the Persian Gulf were primitive to say the least.

Travellers who wished to land at one of the ports along the Gulf were more or less obliged to arrange their own passage on one of the Arab trading vessels, those dhows which are the sole means of maritime transport in that inhospitable region. This we accordingly did, and a couple of weeks after waving farewell to Fenton in Calcutta, we found ourselves in the middle of the Gulf in the company of as villainous a crew of cut-throats as I have encountered in all my life.

I was heartened by the fact that I had no difficulty in conversing with these piratical figures from some Arabian fairy tale, though I must say that the construction of their sentences was occasionally very different from the classical usage – as was almost the whole of their vocabulary. Sigerson, too, sought to master the language, and succeeded to a greater extent than I should have believed possible in so short a time. He seemed to have a natural ear for the nuances of foreign tongues, something which he admitted having possessed from early youth, though he made light of his talents.

So all in all the time passed pleasantly enough, until we landed at the bustling port of Bushire, midway along the Gulf, and said goodbye to our erstwhile shipmates.

Following the plans we had discussed with Fenton and Colonel Stark, we first provided ourselves with native costume, which was by this time almost more familiar to us than serge suiting. The next task was to hire guides and horses, and equip ourselves for the journey across country to Teheran, for there is nothing approaching a railway system in Persia.

The entire journey took us some three or four weeks, as I recall. Once again, I am obliged to dismiss what was a memorable expedition in a very few words, or run the risk of wearying my readers, for there was little that was worth recording, apart from the travelling itself.

We got as far as Shiraz, and there joined a band of merchants bound for Isfahan. As in Tibet, these loose alliances for the purposes of travel are quite common, for the roads are rough, and there are said to be bandits, though I confess we ourselves never encountered any trouble from them.

We managed to make ourselves understood to these men, and they seemed to take us for Arabs, though of a different branch of the race from their own. Neither Sigerson nor I troubled to enlighten them. Indeed, we went along with the mild deception they were practising upon themselves to the extent of joining in their prayers several times a day. I did not think then, nor do I believe now, that we did anything very reprehensible, though I am sure there are those who would disagree. After all, I do not think that a Muslim visitor to London would compromise his religious beliefs by attending a service at any of the churches there.

Arrived at Isfahan, we joined a second caravan headed across the Great Salt Desert, the Dasht-e-Kavir, towards

Teheran. And, some four weeks after first landing in Persia, we came to the capital, and passed through one of the twelve great tiled gates into the city.

Teheran was a curious place. Immediately beyond the gate through which we had entered the city, there was a vast open space, like a football pitch, and beyond that again, a modern railway yard, incongruous in what should have been a scene from Haroun al Raschid. We learnt later that there is only one railway line in all Persia, from Teheran to the town of Shah Abdul Azim, a few miles away – or at least there was then, there may be more these days. Beyond the railway yard the city proper began, a crazy jumble of houses of a western type, which would not have seemed out of place in the suburbs of London or Boston, with as motley a collection of inhabitants as you will find anywhere, for Persia is truly the cross-roads of all the world.

Our friends the merchants gave us directions to the British Legation, an imposing building set in extensive gardens, which stood some two miles from the gate by which we had entered the city.

The guardian at the door looked somewhat askance at our costumes and general appearance, but we had letters of introduction from Fenton and the colonel, which worked wonders. A very short while later, we were ushered into the presence of the military attaché, a Major Wilberforce.

Wilberforce was a very different man from the leathery and alert Colonel Stark. He was a large man, stout with the stoutness that results from regular attendance at the dinner table in the company of the great and the good. It was early evening, and he was dressed for dinner – another dinner, I might as well have said. As we walked into his office, I could have sworn that his lip curled at our dishevelled and travel-stained appearance. He made no remark, though, and shook our hands readily enough.

'Well,' he began, 'and what can I do for you?'

'You will perhaps have had some word from Colonel Stark in Calcutta?' said Sigerson.

'I received a note a couple of days ago,' said Wilberforce in an offhand manner, waving in the general direction of a cabinet that stood in a corner of his office.

Sigerson tried again. 'We have reason to believe that a Prince Igorov, who is, we think, attached in some capacity to the Russian Legation, plans some mischief or the other. Something which will not be to Britain's advantage, that is to say.'

'In Persia?' Wilberforce did not trouble to hide his scepticism. 'I hardly think that very likely, the country is very secure; no danger that the Shah will be overthrown just yet.'

'Let us hope that you are right,' said Sigerson calmly. 'But can you tell us whether this Prince Igorov is in Teheran?'

'He is,' said Wilberforce. 'He has been here for some weeks, and he is indeed staying at their Legation, though in just what capacity I really could not say. We keep an eye on all their chaps, of course, and I can say that Igorov has not been up to anything untoward. In fact, he spends most of his time in the lower quarters of the city, talking to beggars and the like.'

'Indeed?' There was a look of keen interest on Sigerson's face. 'And does that not strike you as significant?'

'Not particularly,' said Wilberforce. 'Should it?'

'Well, it is scarcely the sort of behaviour one would expect of a career diplomat, is it? Could you possibly describe the prince, for we have not actually had the pleasure of meeting him?'

'I can introduce you to him, if you wish,' said Wilberforce, much to my astonishment. 'Or rather,' he added, with a wry look at us, 'I could have done so, had you brought any dress clothes with you, for we shall both be attending an informal reception at the Turkish Embassy shortly.' He tapped a finger on the desk top, as if deep in thought. 'We may be able to arrange something, though,' he said slowly. 'A couple of my colleagues who are much of your size may be prevailed upon – wait here a moment, would you?' and he got to his feet and, without waiting for an answer from us, went out quickly.

Sigerson raised an eyebrow. 'Have we convinced him, think you?'

'No,' said I. 'He thinks us mad, and in true English fashion has to treat us with the greatest possible consideration as a consequence.'

Sigerson laughed. 'Perhaps you are right. But –' and he broke off as Wilberforce returned, followed by two young men, who regarded us with some interest.

'Lieutenant Dyce, Mr Sigerson, may I introduce Mr Brown and Captain Mortimer? I was saying that your dress clothes were lost somewhere in the course of your most interesting journey, and my friends here have kindly offered to donate theirs for this evening.'

We murmured our thanks, and allowed ourselves to be taken off and made respectable. The two young men were indeed much of a size with us, and if Sigerson found Captain Mortimer's trousers a trifle baggy, and if I found Mr Brown's collar a touch tight, well, it was only for one night, and all in a good cause to boot. We had little time to consider the fit, for scarcely had we finished dressing than Wilberforce hauled us off to his carriage.

'We have no invitations,' I reminded him.

'Oh, I shall say you are travellers, arrived at the Legation unexpectedly. The Ambassador is a good fellow, he will make no difficulty there.'

'More to the point,' I continued to Sigerson, 'is it a good idea to allow Igorov to see us, do you think?'

'I do not see why not,' he replied. 'He has never seen us before, remember. If he thinks we are suspicious characters, a danger to him, well, that may prevent his carrying out whatever he has in mind. If not, then he cannot possibly connect us with – with any events of the past.'

'It was more the future I was thinking of. If he can recognize us again it might be dangerous for us.'

'H'mm. I think on balance that it will be worth the risk, in order to get a look at him,' said Sigerson. But there was that in his voice which made me think that his curiosity had got the better of his common sense.

We arrived at the Turkish Embassy and Wilberforce led the way inside. The reception room was crowded; I think every diplomat in Teheran must have been invited.

'Is the prince here yet?' asked Sigerson in a low tone.

Wilberforce glanced round. 'Not yet. I shall have to present you to the Ambassador, first.' He gestured towards the far side of the room.

'The little chap, surrounded by good-looking young men?' I asked with some distaste.

'Don't be fooled by appearances, you cur,' said Wilberforce in a friendly tone. 'Most of the fellows at the Legation would hesitate to get in his way on the polo field. Furthermore, he has the maximum number of wives permitted by his religion, and some two dozen children at the last count.'

'I humbly beg his pardon,' I muttered, as Wilberforce led us across to the Turkish Ambassador.

'You must remember that Islam does not assign women a central role in government, which is why this is an all-male gathering,' Wilberforce told me in a hoarse whisper. 'Ah, Your Excellency! Many thanks for inviting me here. I took the liberty of bringing two friends along, I knew you would not mind. This is Mr Dyce, who is thinking of commencing a career in diplomacy, and wished to take a look at Persia before accepting a posting here. And this is Mr Sigerson, whom Dyce met, as I understand it, on the way here. Mr Sigerson is a Norwegian,' he added, in the dismissive tone the British reserve for discussing foreigners.

'Delighted, delighted!' said the Ambassador. 'A drink? I regret I can offer nothing than orange juice, but it is of the finest.' He snapped his fingers, and a tray of glasses appeared magically. 'Ah,' said the Ambassador to Wilberforce, with a nod to the door, 'more good friends.'

Wilberforce turned and nodded at the two men who were making their way towards the Ambassador. They paid their respects, then turned to us.

'Mr Dyce, Mr Sigerson,' said Wilberforce. 'May I present Count Ulyanov, the Deputy Minister, and Prince Igorov, ah –' and, evidently not knowing Igorov's official title, left it there.

Count Ulyanov was a dapper young man of average height with a neat little moustache. He bowed politely and murmured a greeting in excellent English.

Igorov was altogether different, well over six feet tall, with a great black beard, like those of the Cossacks he led. He clicked his heels together and bowed in the German fashion. 'Delighted, Mr Dyce, and Mr – Sigerson?' He too spoke good English.

Wilberforce, answering the question in the Russian's tone, said, 'Mr Sigerson is a Norwegian.'

'Indeed?' said Igorov, and then to my horror he proceeded to speak to Sigerson in some language which I could not place, I assumed it was Norwegian.

But Sigerson did not turn a hair. He waited until the Prince paused, then replied in the same language, finally remarking, 'However, out of deference to our colleagues, we might be as well to stick to English, do you not think?'

The prince bowed again, and excused himself. As he walked to the far side of the room, I muttered, 'Thank Heaven you could actually speak Norwegian!'

'I had all but exhausted my small vocabulary,' he confessed. 'As luck would have it, Igorov spoke not Norwegian but Swedish, which is quite close. Their borders run close together, you will remember from your geography lessons. So I do not think he will have spotted any deficiencies in my pronunciation and the like, whilst at the same time I ought to have convinced him that I am indeed from Scandinavia.'

'And how came you to know any of the language?' I wanted to know.

'Oh,' said he dismissively, 'I have visited Norway more than once. The salmon fishing, and so forth. More to the point, could you recognize our friend if you saw him again?'

'I scarcely think one could mistake him.'

'Good, for we shall need to follow him, and somewhat more closely than he has been followed thus far. No offence intended, Major.'

'None taken,' said Wilberforce cheerfully. 'You are welcome to do what you will, and I'll give you what help I can. I simply don't have men available to follow everyone who might be acting suspiciously, I'm afraid. Persia is such a quiet, settled sort of place that cloak-and-dagger work is unnecessary.'

'Ah, how true!' said the Turkish Ambassador, who had moved across to us unnoticed. 'As Mr Dyce will find if he accepts a posting here, nothing could be more delightful, eh, Major?'

'Just what I was telling 'em,' said Wilberforce, and the conversation drifted into safer channels, with the remainder of the evening passing uneventfully.

Wilberforce provided us with a couple of cots in a corner of the Legation, telling us that we should be able to draw sufficient funds from the diplomatic petty cash on the following day to enable us to take a room at the English Hotel – after we had visited one of the many western-style tailors' shops, he added, with something of his old disdain for our travelling costumes.

Next day, we did indeed visit the haberdasher's, and engage rooms at the hotel. Then we returned to the Legation, clad respectably enough this time even for Wilberforce, and all three of us took a stroll to the Russian Legation, where Wilberforce showed us the best spot to lurk in order to see who came and went, without ourselves being observed.

'It would be extremely useful if we might have the use of a corner of the Legation, in order to disguise ourselves before we station ourselves here,' said Sigerson.

Wilberforce shook his head. 'Can't be done, I'm afraid – oh, I'd agree like a shot, despite the fact that I don't like this secret work, but the Legation is too public, it would attract attention if two villainous wretches were seen going in and coming out on a regular basis.' He hesitated. 'I tell you what. I have a small private apartment – nothing more than a couple of rooms – not too far away. Comes in handy,' he mumbled, by way of explanation, and neither Sigerson nor I saw fit to ask what it came in handy for.

Wilberforce took us along to the rooms. They could not have suited our purpose better, situated as they were in a nondescript building halfway between our hotel and the Russian Legation. As we went into the lobby, we passed Persians in western dress, an Arab, clearly newly arrived from the desert, in his flowing robes, and an attractive woman of twenty or so, who would not have been out of place in a Paris café.

With a certain amount of reluctance, Wilberforce handed over the keys of the place. Heaven only knows what delicious assignations he was forgoing so that we might have our bolthole – once again, we did not see fit to enquire.

And then the next week or so settled down into a fairly regular, indeed a monotonous, pattern. Sigerson and I rose early, went along to Wilberforce's rooms and changed our western suits for the grimy robes we had worn on the journey to Teheran, then stationed ourselves outside the Russian Legation, hoping to catch a glimpse of Igorov.

I may say that we were inevitably successful in this, for he went out every day, and we duly followed. On one occasion we were obliged to run after his carriage at a discreet distance, only to find that he went to the British Legation! We discovered later that day that he was paying a courtesy call upon the Minister, a fact which Wilberforce had known well enough, but had kept from us as a result of some distorted idea as to what constituted humour.

But for the most part, Igorov went on foot, and he did seem, as Wilberforce had said earlier, to resort to some strange – though not particularly sinister – haunts, seeming mainly interested in the religious side of life in the capital, for he frequently went, not to the mosques which are closed to foreigners, but to some of the religious leaders of the place.

I asked Sigerson what he thought to all this, and he replied, 'Well, I do not think the prince is particularly concerned as to his eventual salvation, so it is something deeper. But as to what –' and he shrugged helplessly, and gave a wry grin.

As I have said, this went on for a week or ten days, and I found that the task palled increasingly with each succeeding day. This was, frankly, not the adventure I had hoped for.

Sigerson, too, seemed to find the job wearisome, for one day at breakfast he remarked to me, 'You know, Dyce, I am capable of the most concentrated bursts of energy, but also of the most pervasive lethargy, and I think that today I am in one of my lethargic moods. Would it bore you terribly to handle the shadowing of Prince Igorov alone? I scarcely think that he will do anything so very staggering that you will be incapable of handling it.'

'I am flattered by your trust in me,' said I, honestly enough, for this was the first time that Sigerson had suggested that I was equal to the task of following the prince alone. And if the reason was not quite as complimentary as it might have been, well, what of that? Here was an opportunity to show that I could work without supervision or assistance.

I went along to the Russian Legation, then, as usual, and as usual Igorov emerged with a cheery word to the attendant at the door, then set off down the road. I followed him to the house of one of the religious teachers, a mullah or imam, as they are known, a place he had often visited before.

I heaved a sigh, for the day was quite chilly – winter was almost upon us – and I knew well enough that Igorov, unless he had changed his habits dramatically in the last two days, would be here until dusk. Still, I had been entrusted with the task of watching him, and watch him I would, so I looked around for a convenient place to settle.

Almost directly opposite the house which Igorov had just entered, there was one of the little coffee houses which correspond to the French cabaret or café. There were a few chairs outside, and I did not see why I should not watch in comfort, so I made my way across to the place.

I sat down, fully expecting the owner, or a waiter, to take my order, but no-one appeared, so I got up and went inside.

The café was deserted, but as I stood there irresolute, a curtain at the back of the little bar opened, and a girl came into the room. She was dark and attractive, but dressed respectably enough in the western fashion, none of the diaphanous draperies that clothe the dancers and other less respectable professions in those parts.

For all her respectable dress, she gave me a smile that could not be mistaken for anything save frank invitation, and I wondered for a moment what sort of an establishment I had inadvertently entered.

But then to my astonishment, she said in a low tone and in good English, 'You are watching the house across the road, yes? You follow the Russian nobleman?'

'Why, yes. That is –'

'Quickly!' she said. 'I have some important news for you. But not out here, we must speak privately,' and she held the curtain open for me.

I did not know what to think. I had no idea that anyone save Sigerson and myself knew of our activities, and here it seemed it was the common gossip of the bazaar! But I should never forgive myself if I failed to gather all the information I might as to the doings of Prince Igorov, so, after a short moment's hesitation, I went through the curtain and into a dark, musty-smelling room.

I could not tell you anything more about the room, for as soon as I stepped inside, someone threw a blanket or something similar over my head, and a brawny pair of arms circled my chest.

I struggled, but it was useless. I could see nothing, and hear only a few words of Arabic, grunted in hoarse voices, two, perhaps three, of them. I was bound – trussed like a turkey, would be nearer the mark – then flung on some sort of cart and driven off.

I seemed to be on that cart for hours, rattling over

cobblestones, then squelching through mud, then more cobbles. At last the cart halted, and I was roughly unloaded on to a hard floor, stood more or less upright and half carried and half dragged up a short flight of steps, before being thrust unceremoniously through a doorway – I knew it was a doorway for the jamb of the door bruised my shoulder as I crashed against it. Then, before I had time to realize what was happening, much less do anything about it, my bonds were untied, and my captors left me alone, locking the door after them.

As soon as I had gathered my scattered wits, I threw off the rug or sack that was still over my head, and made a dash for the door, but it was hopeless, it was solid wood, with a huge lock to it, and it was firmly closed against me.

Then, more calmly, I bethought me to take a look at my prison. I was in a small, but not cramped, room, with a cot in one corner. The only light came from a tiny window, a fanlight I should have said, were this England, high up towards the ceiling. Even if I moved the cot and stood on it, I could not reach the window, and if I did manage to reach it, I could never get through it. Still, it was worth a try, better failure than simply sitting here awaiting whatever fate my captors – captor, rather, for it was now only too clear to me that Igorov was behind this – had in mind for me. I tried to move the cot, but it was bolted to the floor. Evidently the room had been used for a similar nefarious purpose before today.

There was nothing to be done but wait. Towards evening, a sort of trapdoor in the bottom of the main door opened, and food was pushed through for me, plenty of it, and well enough cooked, though at first I hesitated to taste it, thinking it might be drugged. Then I thought, they have me at their mercy in any event, so what could they gain by drugging me now? I ate heartily, and without ill effects, then, astounding though it is, went off into a sound sleep.

I was fed again in the morning, and in the evening of that second day. By this time I was heartily tired of the whole thing. I endeavoured to attract the attention of my attendants when they put my meals through the door, but they refused to speak in return, nor did they take any notice when, my temper strained beyond limitation, I banged for half an hour on the door with the tray which had held my breakfast.

I spent a second night in my cell, and this time I could not sleep, but lay there blaming myself for my stupidity.

The dawn came, lighting up a corner of my room, but today, just as I was hoping for some breakfast, and perhaps some explanation, there was a terrific commotion outside my door.

I stood ready, thinking that some violence was intended against me at last. There was a last crash from outside, a rattle of the key in the lock, and the door was flung open. I braced myself for the expected attack, but it never came.

Instead, I heard Sigerson's voice, bitter with anger, saying, 'Well, Lieutenant Dyce, a very pretty hash you have made of things!'

13

'Call me Selim'

'Well, really!' said Sigerson, as I staggered out into the daylight. 'It does seem as if all my associates must needs be susceptible to feminine wiles of the most obvious sort. A winsome smile, and the work of days, weeks, even years, goes out of the window at once. Heaven only knows what effect a glimpse of a shapely ankle might produce.'

'Really, sir,' I said, with as much dignity as I could muster, 'that is most uncalled for. The lady assured me that she had some information concerning Igorov, and that was the only, the sole, reason for my dropping my guard in what was, I freely confess, a most reckless manner.'

'Indeed?' Sigerson's tone was a touch more sympathetic now. 'That means that the owner of the café must have been in on it. We must return there, and try to catch the scent once more.' He smiled at me. 'But I am forgetting my manners. Lieutenant Dyce, this is the man you have to thank for your rescue, Monsieur Selim Barakat.'

'Please, call me Selim.' A tall young man, with olive skin, dark hair and a moustache which might have been pen-cilled on with kohl, stepped out of the shadows, bowed, and extended his hand to me.

'Monsieur Barakat – Selim, then, if you insist upon it – is attached to the Turkish Legation. You may have noticed him at the reception a week ago?'

'Ah –'

'There were many people there,' said Selim, with a deprecating smile. 'It was difficult to remember everyone.' He looked at Sigerson, and the smile broadened. 'Unless you have been trained to do so,' he added.

'Well,' said Sigerson, with the air of a man who would change the subject, 'the next task is to question the café owner – though frankly I do not hold out much hope from that quarter – and try to cut Igorov's trail.'

'That is the second time you have used that phrase,' said I. 'Do I conclude that he has decamped whilst I have been locked up here?'

'And whilst we have been looking for you,' said Sigerson bitterly, 'yes.'

'I can only repeat that I acted for the best.'

Selim snapped out a command in a language that was unfamiliar to me, and a couple of soldiers in Turkish uniform stepped forward and stood to attention. 'There is little purpose questioning the ruffians who kidnapped Lieutenant Dyce and held him here,' said Selim, 'for they would recognize only the money they were paid for the task. But the café owner may respond to our questions.' He nodded at one of his men, who led the way out into the street, down a mean alley, and into that self-same street in which I had been abducted. The very café itself was just across the road.

'Why!' said I, 'I would have sworn that I had been taken miles away.'

'A circular journey,' said Selim.

Sigerson added in a bored tone, 'A simple device. And now let us see what my genial host might have to tell us.'

We entered the little coffee shop, and the proprietor, a short man of fifty or so, came forward with an obsequious smile on his face. I stepped forward, so that he might get a good look at me, but there was no trace of guilt or recognition apparent on his face. Clearly he had not been directly involved in the attack upon me.

'If you will forgive me?' Selim murmured, and before we had realized what he intended, he and the two soldiers seized the café owner gently but firmly and took him behind the bar, and through that curtain with which I was already acquainted.

Sigerson looked at me, and raised an eyebrow. 'Perhaps a trifle unorthodox, but I have no doubt Monsieur Barakat's methods will prove most effective. Ah,' he cried, as Selim emerged from the den at the back, 'finished already?'

Selim shrugged. 'He knows nothing. He was paid – well paid – to close the café and absent himself for the day.'

'I thought the place seemed empty,' I remarked.

Selim nodded. 'The only woman in the place is his wife, and from his description she is not the houri who led the lieutenant astray. Of course, if you would like to see her –'

'That will hardly be necessary,' said Sigerson with a laugh.

'He says that they threatened her,' added Selim, 'and that he would have refused but for that. It may be true. Who can say?' He shrugged again. 'A handful of gold buys a poor man's conscience.' He became businesslike, turned to his soldiers and dismissed them with a curt word. They saluted and marched away. 'I think we might venture on a cup of his coffee,' Selim continued. 'I hardly think he will poison us now.' He called an order to the frightened proprietor, who hastened to obey, and led the way to a quiet corner.

'Now, we must discuss the best course of action,' said Sigerson, 'and as quickly as may be.'

'But how on earth did you find me?' I wanted to know. 'And how came the two of you to be acquainted?'

Sigerson waved a hand dismissively. 'We really have little time for trifles of that sort.'

'I am not sure,' said Selim thoughtfully. 'In the east we do not have the same need to hasten as you do, yet perhaps we get there just as fast. Lieutenant Dyce is naturally curious as to just what happened.'

'It is quite irrelevant,' snapped Sigerson waspishly, in a tone so far removed from his usual politeness that I raised an eyebrow at Selim, who grinned.

'But it was so amusing!' Selim told me. 'You see, I had been following you –'

'And why, pray?'

Selim gave another oriental shrug. 'It seemed likely to prove interesting – and it did, yes? Anyway, Mr Sigerson here had observed me – and others – on the trail, and decided to set a little trap.'

'Ah, so that is why you sent me out alone, as a decoy?'

Sigerson snorted audibly, and devoted his attention to the sticky sweetmeat, immersed in a tall glass of iced water, which the proprietor had just brought him.

Selim went on, 'When I myself set out to follow, I saw at once that Mr Sigerson was following someone else, someone I knew nothing about.'

'Igorov's men!' said I.

Selim nodded. 'Evidently. I thought, this looks like good sport, and set off to follow Mr Sigerson.'

'I never saw him,' Sigerson confessed, 'for I thought there was only one man, and I had marked him already. When you entered the café and spoke to the girl, I settled down to watch what might happen – I was suspicious, for I had seen the man who was trailing you go into the back lane behind the café. I did not know that Selim had settled down to watch me in turn.' He broke off to wave away a beggar who had wandered into the place, and was making himself objectionable with his whining.

Selim took up the tale. 'When Mr Sigerson thought you

had been gone too long, he entered the café himself. I, no longer able to contain my curiosity, went in after him. We had never been introduced, you see, and besides it was dark inside, and consequently Mr Sigerson was – initially, at least – under the impression that I was one of the gang who had made off with you, and that I proposed to do the same to him.'

'Indeed!' said I, delighted. 'So it appears we both made an error of judgement.' The beggar was now standing at my shoulder, and I dismissed him with a firm, 'Imshi! Clear off!' before asking, 'And what happened then?'

'This is not getting us any nearer our main goal,' said Sigerson.

Selim rubbed his left arm. 'He fights like a tiger, your Mr Sigerson,' he told me ruefully.

'You are quite proficient in the noble art yourself,' said Sigerson magnanimously. He threw back his head and laughed aloud. 'By the time each of us had established his bona fides to the satisfaction of the other, the trail was quite cold. Only Selim's good offices, and the generous application of palm-oil, enabled us to find your prison today. Almost three full days wasted,' he added with a return of the acrimony he had shown earlier. 'Igorov must have left the city as soon as he knew we were occupied looking for you, and as a result has almost three clear days' start on us. Moreover, we have not the slightest notion as to which direction he has chosen.'

'Come, things may not be so bad,' said Selim, and was about to say more when the beggar, evidently quite determined not to leave such an august company empty handed, approached him. Selim waved a hand in elegant dismissal.

'I offend the Frankish milords,' said the beggar, speaking a villainous English in a curious high whine, 'do I also offend the Turkish bey?'

Selim laughed. 'Blessed are they that give alms in the

name of Allah,' he quoted, 'for it shall return five-fold as an ear of corn, and every ear shall bear a hundred grains.' He reached into the pocket of his elegant trousers. 'Take, then be gone, son of an incontinent camel.'

The beggar flung himself onto his knees, and took Selim's hand in both his grimy paws. When he rose and opened his hand, there was silver, not just copper, therein, and he almost ran out, calling down blessings on Selim, his wives and his offspring unto the tenth generation.

'If you would excuse me a moment?' Selim rose, looked about him, and went out through a back door into heaven knew what sordid purlieu.

Sigerson leaned over the table. 'As you will have gathered,' he told me in a low tone, 'this fellow Barakat is an agent of the Turkish secret service, and that is why he was interested in Igorov. Fortunately, relations between Turkey and Britain are excellent at the moment, and he has given me every assistance in the search for you – indeed, it would be true to say that, without him, you would still be a prisoner.'

'I wonder how long they had planned to keep me locked up?'

Sigerson shrugged. 'Until they became bored, I imagine,' he said cheerfully. 'The longer the better, so far as Igorov was concerned, for it meant we should be prevented that much longer from following him. Well, we must possess our souls in patience, until Selim deigns to share with us the information which his messenger has just brought.'

'His messenger?'

'My dear fellow!' said Sigerson, shaking his head sadly. 'Ah, Selim. And what news have you?'

Selim laughed. 'I should have known that my Turkish carrier pigeon would not escape the gaze of the Frankish hawk. News, indeed! Good news, my friends: we have found him. He heads west and by south across the desert, and his ultimate goal is Mecca.'

Sigerson and I stared at one another in silence for a long moment. Then Sigerson asked, 'You are certain?'

'Absolutely. He has taken a dragoman, and porters, and paid them well for their silence. But the dragoman must know the destination, to calculate the food and so forth needed for the journey. And the dragoman has a wife, and the wife has a brother, and the brother has a wife who has a cousin who is one of my men.' He smiled at us.

'Good Lord!' said I. 'No wonder you were able to find me!'

Selim's dusky face flushed, for all the world like an Indian maiden who has been paid a flowery compliment. 'He specified Mecca, but the dragoman, not being very familiar with the desert – and perhaps being a little over-fond of that wife of his – undertook only to go as far as Baghdad with him. Igorov must find another guide there, and that will take time, so it may be possible to catch him before he sets off on the next stage of his journey.'

'It will be better merely to follow, to see exactly what he is about before we act,' said the practical Sigerson. 'The really interesting question must be, why Mecca? We know that Igorov has been speaking to a religious teacher here in Teheran, the man whose house lies opposite. And now he travels to Mecca. Why, I wonder? Does Islam appeal to him? I beg leave to doubt it.'

'Remember that in Mecca he will find the true Islam,' said Selim. 'The variety found here is Shi'ia, and that is – well,' and he made a little moue of distaste. 'And yet I think you are right, I too distrust this sudden enlightenment – and besides, should he not have taken the road to Damascus in that case?' He threw back his head and laughed, then grew serious again. 'He is up to something, no doubt about it. And the fact that he is meddling with my religion offends me.'

'He may have lied, knowing that his guide would not take him so far, and knowing also that we should ask questions,' I said.

'Well, that is possible. But there is only one way to determine what he is doing,' said Sigerson, 'and that is for us to follow him to Mecca, or to Baghdad in the first instance.'

'You are right,' said Selim. He pushed his coffee cup away, and made ready to stand up. 'If we begin the preparations now, we can leave early tomorrow morning.'

'I meant, of course, that Dyce and I would follow him, my dear fellow,' said Sigerson.

'And I, my dear fellow, mean that the three of us should follow him,' answered Selim.

Sigerson shook his head quickly. 'It is our quarrel.'

'Here in Persia, perhaps. In England or Russia, undoubtedly. But Mecca, though on the fringes of the Ottoman Empire, is nonetheless part of that Empire, and thus within my territory. Baghdad most certainly is my concern.'

'There will be danger.'

'I have four sons,' said Selim. 'If I enter Paradise, my line will continue. And doubtless you yourselves have made similar provisions.'

'My own contribution to posterity has been more modest,' said Sigerson, 'while young Dyce here has been too busy to bother with anything of the kind. It is a kind offer, but I really cannot permit it. Think of the reproaches from those four sons were you not to return. How should I face that?'

'That is your last word?'

'Absolutely. Dyce and I shall leave tomorrow. Alone.'

'The winter has just recently begun,' mused Selim, 'so

travel will not be too difficult yet. You ought to cross the border into the Turkish administration – what – a week from today? So I assure you that a week from tomorrow, you will be arrested. A couple of days in a Turkish prison – not the most hospitable of places, I fear – and you will be passed on to the British Consul with a curt note that you are to be sent back to England at once, and will thenceforth be regarded as persona non grata. Or should that be personas? Or even personae?' he asked anxiously.

The finer points of Latin syntax were clearly not uppermost in Sigerson's mind at that moment. His face showed a mixture of impotent rage and bafflement, barely suppressed, and badly suppressed, but suppressed nevertheless. 'You would do that?' he asked at last.

Selim nodded. 'I should regret it, of course. It would be much better if you could go to Mecca with me, and investigate this rogue's doings. But, if I must go alone –' and he shrugged.

The fact that Sigerson did not grind his teeth audibly is a magnificent testimony to the achievements of the English educational system. Speaking with an effort, he said, 'You will place yourself under my command? You will restrain that youthful exuberance which has already jeopardized my – our – mission?'

'Provided that it does not conflict with my duty to my superiors, my country, or the government I have the honour to serve, I will do so gladly,' said Selim, holding out his hand.

Sigerson shook the proffered hand and smiled briefly. 'How soon can we start?'

14

Mecca

Selim evidently had some considerable influence at his Legation, for we were indeed able to set out early next morning, complete with a dragoman – that curious oriental compound of guide, adviser, confidant and man of business – a dozen mule drivers and their charges to carry our baggage, and six heavily armed Turkish soldiers.

Sigerson had ventured to enquire whether such a large caravan was strictly necessary, and I confess that I had raised an eyebrow as well, but Selim assured us that our party was still not by any means so numerous as to positively guarantee our safety. The mountains, he said, were full of bandits, and moreover the approaching winter would itself add to the difficulty of the journey. The mules were needed to transport the large quantities of tinned foodstuffs we should have to take, for such inns as there might be along the way were not to be relied upon, and there were none of any kind in the mountains.

Convinced by these arguments, Sigerson and I held our peace, and let Selim get on with the arrangements, with the result, as I say, that all was ready for our departure next day.

Once again I am placed in the awkward position of having to decide between writing a lengthy guide to part of Asia Minor, or dismissing a lengthy, memorable and not entirely comfortable journey in a few lines. The journey itself may have formed no part of our main scheme, or adventure, but nevertheless it was one which I shall not soon forget.

Our first day or so was spent in crossing a part of that Dasht-e-Kavir which we had already traversed on the way into Teheran. At that season it was very far from the average Englishman's idea of a desert, for it resembled nothing so much as a rugby field which has seen hard use after a week of continuous rain. Then up into the Zagros Mountains, the track getting steeper, narrower and rockier as we went.

Winter was beginning to take hold in good earnest now, and we were soon compelled to cease all idle conversation as we went, and battle, with heads bent down, against the sleet and snow driven at us by the bitter winds. We had cause then to thank Selim for his preparations, for I do not know what we should have done without the furs and heavy travelling cloaks he had equipped us with. The soldiers, too, were amply provided for, and so were some of the more provident muleteers, but some of the poor fellows, either from a lack of foresight akin to that of the foolish virgins, or from simple lack of the wherewithal to buy warm clothing, faced those appalling conditions in nothing more than thin cotton jackets. On more than one occasion we had quite literally to set some poor half-frozen mule driver by the fireside so that he might thaw out at the end of our day's march. And this despite the fact that the sun often shone brilliantly overhead for the whole day! But it was an illusory brightness, with no sort of warmth to be felt in it.

Although the track is difficult and dangerous, it is – in the right season for travelling, at any rate – quite well patronized, and there are inns or settlements strung out along the way, save in the most inhospitable stretches, so that we did not have to spend more than one or two nights outside, thank Heaven. And we never did encounter any bandits, to my secret disappointment. I suspect that, like all sensible men, they had found snug quarters for the winter.

After a week or so of this, we noticed that we were travelling gradually down, instead of up. Selim assured us that we should be in Baghdad in a very few days, and this proved correct.

As this was Selim's home ground, we left the immediate enquiries very much to him, and in a very short time he had discovered that Igorov had joined a caravan bound for Medina, and had been gone three days.

'They cannot have got very far,' I said eagerly, 'for they will travel at the speed of the slowest camel. If we get fresh horses, we ought to be able to catch up with them very quickly.'

But Selim shook his head. 'And then what? I have no doubt that the prince has a passport and permits, all will be as it should. True, I might have him arrested and deported, but then another agent could easily be sent to complete the task, whatever it may be. Far better to travel after them, we could catch up a little, I think, a day or so, in order that there will not be too great a delay when we arrive, but far enough behind not to attract attention to ourselves. I shall start to search for guides and provisions.'

The last remark referred to the fact that we had by this time lost our original guide and the mule drivers. Being doubtful as to whether they possessed the detailed knowledge needed for a desert crossing – a doubt which I may say that I shared, in view of the failure of some of their number to bring along as much as a decent coat for a winter trek through the mountains – they had taken their pay and set off back through those mountains to Teheran. Selim accordingly left us, and went to seek out local men for the task.

He returned in great glee, to say that not only had he found suitable men, but that he had been approached by a couple of merchants desirous of travelling to Medina with us. These men had intended to reach Baghdad in time to join that caravan by which Igorov had departed, but some delay had prevented their doing so, and they were now sitting in a caravanserai alternately bemoaning their fate, and asking if anyone might be going in that general direction.

'Will they not slow us down?' I had to ask.

'I think not,' said Selim. 'Their camels are in good heart, and there are not too many of them. But they will be useful in case of trouble, and moreover the presence of merchants will serve to allay any suspicion of our party.'

Between ourselves, I rather suspect that these merchants had contributed to the expenses of outfitting the soldiers who were still with us, which was, I suppose, fair enough, as we were giving them the benefit of our protection.

Having told us about the merchants, Selim had another proposition to put to us, this time of a more delicate nature. 'It might be as well,' said he, 'if you were to pass as Muslims yourselves. Although there have been plenty of westerners who have crossed the desert – and visited Mecca, come to that – they have usually done so in disguise, for there are many fanatics who would take exception to your presence here.'

By this time both Sigerson and I were not so much tanned as weather stained. Then we had both grown beards of a sort during the journey, for the facilities for one's morning toilet were rudimentary in the mountains. So, with our baggy trousers and long travelling cloaks, we passed easily enough for natives.

Our only concern was how Selim's men might react to our joining in their devotions, but he assured us that they were all hand picked by him, that they were soldiers first and foremost and thus had the practical approach of soldiers, and finally that, provided we remained at the back of the assembly so that they could not actually see what we did, they would have no objection whatever to our being there. He further told me privately, Sigerson being busy elsewhere, that there were still plenty of eunuchs in Byzantium, but that none of his soldiers had the slightest inclination to join their unmanly ranks, a fate he had categorically assured them lay in wait should they betray us by so much as a contemptuous curl of the lip.

For myself, although I naturally have my own convictions, I am not a fervent devotee of any particular doctrine, and could see nothing wrong in joining in the worship of the Creator, whatever form it might take. And although I obviously could not, and did not, discuss the matter with Sigerson, I got the impression that he took much the same view as I did. I do know that we had no difficulty or unpleasantness in that direction.

And now began what will form – thank Heaven – the last of my 'epic journey in a single paragraph' descriptions.

For several weeks we struggled over the desert. I lost all sense of direction, and not direction alone but time as well, for there ensued a succession of identical hot days, with the wind blowing the sand into our faces, followed by identical bitterly cold nights, until they merged one into another.

We had no difficulty with the desert tribes. Nominally part of the Ottoman Empire, in practice they acknowledge no leaders but their own local chiefs. Selim told us that they would happily rob a small party of travellers, but preferred to negotiate with larger, well armed groups such as ourselves, accepting a modest tribute in exchange for accompanying us from one side of their own territory to the other. It is a regular source of income for them, and they run it most efficiently. Indeed, I often thought that, if those arid lands had contained anything that mankind might esteem highly, these desert people might take their place among the capitalists of London or New York. Protected by these men, we could sleep easily at night, after a good meal and some interesting conversation.

Selim made a point of asking casually if there had been any other caravans going that way recently, and the answers showed that we were not too far behind Igorov.

It was in the evenings, by the fire, that Selim told us much about his own country and religion. He himself was of the larger Sunni, or orthodox, sect, and consequently never felt entirely at home in Persia, which is the home of the Shi'ia sect, a more fanatical group. Selim told us something of the differences in point of doctrine between the two, but he said that, try as he might, he could not see what Igorov might have found in either branch of the faith – nor yet in any conflict between the two, for in practice they co-exist happily – to interest him.

'Well, then,' asked Sigerson – we could speak freely, and in English, for the merchants sat together at another fire, with the soldiers at a third and the local tribesman at a fourth – 'well, then, could it be some political weakness that he seeks to exploit? These desert tribes, for instance, could he be wanting to stir them up against the Porte?'

Selim shook his head. 'There is, at this very moment, some small unpleasantness with some of the tribesmen nearer Mecca, but nothing very serious.'

'Nothing approaching a civil war?'

Selim laughed. 'The desert tribes are not sufficiently numerous to be a serious danger in that regard. Though they are difficult to fight with regular troops, as they travel light, and thus move far and fast, thereby avoiding the regular forces.'

'And what of the broader political picture?' asked Sigerson.

'I cannot see that there is anything specific,' said Selim with a shrug. 'The Ottoman Empire has been in existence a good many years, and consequently some of its manifestations are not exactly modern. It is true that pressure for reform is building, but that is from within.'

'But it could be exploited?'

'Perhaps. But not, I do assure you, from the remoteness of Mecca, spiritual centre of Islam though it may be. Then again, the Porte has good relations with almost every nation of importance, with Britain, Germany –'

'Ah, with Germany?'

'Of course. There are German engineers not too far away from us now – comparatively speaking, of course – building a railway.'

'H'mm.' Sigerson stared into the fire.

'You do not suppose that there is anything to be made of that?' I asked him. 'We too have good relations with Germany. Why, our own Queen is related to the Kaiser.'

Sigerson smiled. 'And yet, if rumour be true, there have been one or two – family quarrels, shall we say? There might be something there, possibly. But what could it be?'

'Gentlemen,' I said, 'we have been over all this many times, with no success. Can we please change the subject? Selim, before we set off from Baghdad, you said that westerners had visited Mecca. Now, I have always been under the impression that the city was strictly forbidden to foreigners like us. Is that not so?'

'Strictly speaking, yes. But in practice, foreigners are usually tolerated, if their behaviour is modest and dignified. Have you never heard of Mr Herman Bicknell?'

I shook my head. Sigerson frowned, and said, 'The name is vaguely familiar, but I cannot quite place it. If only I had my index here!'

Selim went on, 'Some years ago, Sir Richard Burton, whose name most certainly will be familiar to both of you, visited Mecca in disguise, and wrote a book about it, stressing the very great dangers he had run in so doing, and counselling his readers on no account to attempt the same deception. Soon after, Mr Bicknell, who perhaps had not read Sir Richard's account, took a steamer to Jeddah, and walked quite openly and without any disguise into Mecca. He engaged the first man he met as a guide, looked round the sights – apparently without feeling any sort of emotion – then on his return to London he wrote a letter to *The Times*, saying that the place was quite interesting, though you would not think so from the description he gave, and recommending anyone who happened to be passing to drop in for a look round.'

'Did he really?' I asked, laughing.

'Oh, yes. One of your true English eccentrics. I myself have seen the letter, Sir Richard cut it from *The Times* and kept it. He never forgave Bicknell, who had, he thought, damaged his reputation as a fearless adventurer.'

'You knew Burton, then?' asked Sigerson.

'I would not say I knew him, but I called upon him once or twice. He ended his days in Damascus, as you may be aware.'

'And so you mean that there is no real risk?' I asked. 'That the dangers have been exaggerated?'

'I would not entirely go so far as to say that,' said Selim circumspectly. 'Provided you are with me, of course, there will be no difficulty, although you will not be able to go inside the mosques or other holy places. Still, there are fanatics – as in all religions – and it will be as well if you do not draw attention to yourselves.'

'I wonder, could Igorov have been prompted by some desire to emulate Burton and the others?' I said. 'Is his visit to Mecca sheer bravado, to show that a Russian traveller can go anywhere an Englishman can?'

Sigerson shook his head. 'It would be comforting to think as much,' he said, 'but that does not accord well with the broad impression which I have formed of the prince. No, he is up to something, you may depend upon that. But what?'

And on that questioning note, our discussions would end, as we sought our blankets.

Three weeks, four, and we came to the city of Medina, where we parted company with our friends the merchants. We had not seen anything of that local unrest which Selim had mentioned, it was evidently on no large scale, and there occurred nothing of interest on the last stage of the journey, the short ride from Medina to Mecca.

For all Selim's reassurances, I felt a touch of trepidation – not entirely unpleasant, I confess – when we saw our goal shimmering in the distance, and I felt far more like the adventurous Burton than the prosaic and pedestrian Bicknell as we rode through the great gate into the ancient and holy city of Mecca.

15

Jeddah to Suakin

I had expected that Mecca would be crowded to overflow-
ing with the pious faithful, for it is the duty of every
Muslim to make the pilgrimage to Mecca, the Hadj, at
least once in his life if he can. But the city was all but
deserted, and Selim explained that the Hadj would not
take place for another month or two yet, and that when it
did take place one would be hard pressed to find a bed in
the entire city.

As it was, we rode along streets where the only sign of
life was the dust blowing into our faces, and thought the
place very animated if we encountered a couple of the
locals leaning on a street corner, passing the time for all the
world like Southsea landladies wishing the winter away,
and hoping that the trippers might arrive early that spring.

It was late afternoon when we arrived, and we secured
accommodation with no difficulty. Selim said that it might
be as well if Sigerson and I stayed in our room, while he
asked for news of Igorov. Sigerson chafed slightly at this,
but I told him it was probably for the best, and he did not
press the matter.

Selim did not return until late in the evening, by which time
I, too, was eager to hear what he might have discovered.

'We have just missed him again!' said he, a look of
vexation on his handsome face. 'Just! He arrived here three

days ago, spent the whole of yesterday talking to yet another holy man, and then they rode off out of the city together just this morning.'

'And what sort of a holy man?' Sigerson wanted to know.

'One of the Shi'ia teachers, a man who had lived here for the past few years. His neighbours tolerated him because they thought him slightly mad, and as you know we are bidden to look after those whom Allah has seen fit to afflict in that fashion. He was apparently a Dervish.'

'Indeed?'

Selim nodded, and his expression cleared. 'However, all is not lost, for I have found where they went.'

'To Jeddah,' said Sigerson in a matter of fact tone.

Selim looked surprised. 'That is so. But how could you know?'

'Well, he did not return to Medina, or we should have seen him, and Jeddah is the only other place of any importance nearby. But that is not by any means the only reason, and you yourself gave the explanation in one of your very interesting talks about the difference between the Sunnis and the Shi'ites. Doubtless you will recollect the point to which I refer, Dyce?'

I racked my brains to remember what Selim had said as to arguments over doctrinal exegeses between the major and minor branches of Islam.

When the Prophet began to preach the faith, his first convert and staunchest follower was his son-in-law, Ali. The main difference between the Sunnis and the Shi'ites is that while the Sunnis hold Ali in high esteem, the Shi'ites give him a rank equal, or indeed superior, to that of the Prophet himself. They believe that the Imams descended from Ali have a special divine mission, that the last of these Imams will be the Mahdi, the Shi'ia Messiah who will lead the Muslims to glorious victory.

Now, in 1848 a boy named Mohammed Ahmed was born at Dongola in the Sudan, which was then under Egyptian control. He worked for a time for the Egyptian civil service, then tried his hand at slave-trading, and finally announced that he was the Mahdi, come to lead his people. The fanatical Dervishes of the Sudan believed him, and rose against their Egyptian overlords.

Egypt at that time was in financial ruin, thanks to the excesses of Khedive Ismail, and the British, owed money by Ismail, had moved in to restore the country to a sound footing. The small British garrison at Khartoum in the Sudan, commanded by General Gordon, was unable to withstand the onslaught of the Mahdi's hordes. In 1885 Khartoum fell, and Gordon was butchered.

By this time, in 1893, the Mahdi was dead, and his successor the Khalifa reigned in his stead. But the fanatical and bloodthirsty Dervishes of the Sudan refused to believe that the Mahdi was dead, they thought he was merely in hiding, waiting to appear on the day on which the world would end.

'He has gone to the Sudan!' I said. 'He plans to stir up the tribesmen, to – to launch an invasion of Egypt, perhaps.'

'It is too fantastic,' said Selim, with a quick shake of his head.

'Nay,' said Sigerson, 'I believe it is exactly as Dyce suggests. It is the best chance he has encountered thus far. In Tibet, he was – or would have been – frustrated as much by the authorities being kindly disposed to Britain as by any efforts of ours. Persia and the Ottoman Empire, both stable regimes, offered little scope for his devilry. But the Sudan is a very different matter. The defeat of Gordon was less than a decade ago, recent enough to be fresh in the minds of the people, to make them susceptible to the suggestion that they are invincible.'

'But the Khalifa's forces could not hope to conquer Egypt!' cried Selim. 'Poorly equipped, untrained tribesmen against regular soldiers? It would make no sense.'

'They might do a good deal of damage before they were stopped, though,' I pointed out.

'Moreover,' added Sigerson, 'the real question is not whether the Sudanese could conquer Egypt – for the answer is almost certainly that they could not – but whether other nations would see fit to embroil themselves in the matter. The French, for example, have long cast envious eyes on Egypt. Indeed, it is only their failure to support Britain's suppression of a revolt led by a man whose name I forget, in a year which escapes me for the moment, which has prevented France ruling Egypt jointly with Britain.'

'It was the Arabi revolt, in 1882,' I put in.

Sigerson raised an eyebrow, looking slightly irked at being thus upstaged.

'My eldest brother took an honourable part in that campaign,' I explained.

'Quite so. It is not too fanciful to suggest that a war involving the whole of Europe might be the consequence of a skirmish on the southern borders of Egypt.'

'With Russia waiting to seize the wreckage?' I asked.

Sigerson nodded. 'It is therefore imperative that – I had almost said "we" – follow at once, but I really feel some hesitation about allowing either of you to accompany me, for the Khalifa has the reputation of being an even madder, more bloodthirsty devil than his instructor, the Mahdi.'

'You will have difficulty preventing our going with you,' I told him.

'Selim?'

'You do not speak Arabic well enough yet to pass for a native, I fear. And that would guarantee a lingering and painful death in the Sudan. So there is really no question of my remaining behind, even if it were not my clear duty to my country. Remember that the Turkish lands lie along part of the Egyptian borders, so that trouble in Egypt would imply trouble in the Ottoman Empire. The Sultans have cast lustful eyes on the waters of the Nile before now, so the army I have the honour to serve in would indubitably receive its marching orders.'

Sigerson accepted his defeat gracefully, and we retired soon after, in anticipation of an early start next day.

Before we actually set out, Selim insisted that we divest ourselves of anything that might mark us out as Christians or westerners. It would, he assured us, be difficult enough to escape detection and arrest in the Sudan, but we were under no obligation to make it entirely impossible. Sigerson, it appeared, had nothing in the way of personal possessions to begin with, and I had not many, a miniature of my parents and the like, and these were left for safe keeping with one of Selim's friends, with a note as to their disposition in the event that I should fail to return to claim them. This obliging friend also provided us with a large sum of money in gold and silver, saying that we stood in need of friends where we were bound.

Selim ordered his soldiers to return to Baghdad, saying that they could not help, and might possibly hinder, the task that lay ahead of us. They complained bitterly, for I think they had some notion of launching an invasion of the Sudan, in the firm conviction that the six of them together with the three of us would together be the equal of the Khalifa's army. Still, they went at last, with a bad grace, and tears in their eyes at being parted from Selim, and then we too were ready to leave.

From Mecca to Jeddah is no great distance, and it was not long before we entered the old port. The inhabitants of Jeddah, from being in almost constant contact with the outside world – for the port is a busy one – regard themselves as far more cosmopolitan than the citizens of Mecca, and very superior to the tribes of the surrounding desert. Regrettably, this superiority manifests itself in an arrogance towards strangers which I soon found irksome. Even more regrettably, it emphatically does not manifest itself in any desire to cleanse the city's streets, which are the filthiest and vilest I have ever walked along.

Still, the presence of so many strangers did mean that we attracted not the slightest attention, and in any case we did not remain in the place for any longer than it took to make enquiries at the docks.

The fourth or fifth man whom we questioned told us that his brother – not his cousin, for a wonder! – had indeed contracted to take two men such as we described across the Gulf to Suakin in the Sudan. He told us, without being asked, that his brother, having a large family to provide for, had charged double the usual rate, as conditions in the Sudan were unstable in the extreme, and added significantly that he too had a large family.

We took the hint, and soon found ourselves on his dhow in the Gulf. The captain was inclined to be sociable, and readily told us all he knew of the present state of the Sudan. The Sudanese, he said, were very suspicious of all strangers, the rule of the Mahdi, and later the Khalifa, having induced in them a fear akin to that experienced by the citizens of France during the Terror, though the captain, in the blunt fashion of sailors, expressed it by a more earthy simile. Anyone who did not really have to go there, he said with a sidelong look, should avoid the place.

By way of allaying any suspicions which the captain might have, Selim told him that we had business with the local governor of Suakin.

'Ah,' said the captain, 'the Emir?'

'Yes,' Selim told him, 'that is the man we seek, do you know him?'

The captain laughed. 'Is it likely, sirs? No, but I know of him, and he is somewhat less crazy than many of them. His hospitality is noted, and strangers are well received at his palace. Usually,' he added as an afterthought.

Sigerson gave me a significant look. 'So it is likely that any strangers who had landed there recently would have gone to see this Emir?'

'Noblemen, men of quality, certainly.'

We arrived at Suakin, a place whose ramshackle wooden wharves and jetties seemed ill-suited to such a bustling port, the major port of the Sudan, or at least it was in those days. There were a good many soldiers wandering about the docks, sullen-looking fellows, heavily armed, looking closely at all who passed them.

On the principle that attack is the best form of defence, we marched boldly up to some of the fiercest looking of these men, and demanded that they escort us to the palace of the Emir.

This they did, and a short time after we were being ushered in to the presence of the great man himself. He was an elderly man, as tall as Sigerson himself, and as lean and ascetic looking, with a great hawk's beak of a nose. For all that he was the representative of a bloodthirsty lunatic, the Emir had a penetrating manner, and a sardonic sense of humour. He spoke a classical Arabic as well as the local variants, and in accordance with our pre-arranged design, Selim informed him that we were three zealots, sworn enemies of all foreigners and infidels, and that whilst in Mecca we had got upon the scent of one who was not only a foreigner and an infidel but a dangerous traitor to boot, a man who had eluded our vigilance for long enough to get to Jeddah, and thence to the Sudan, where, we were certain, he planned some harm to the Khalifa and his loyal servants.

The Emir listened to all this in silence, and his eyes narrowed as he listened. When Selim had told his tale, and described Igorov, the Emir said, 'Yes, there was such a man. He came to me yesterday, together with a – a holy man,' – the pause was only slight, but it was clear that Igorov's companion had failed to impress the Emir favourably – 'and they had some tale of being divinely inspired to travel to Khartoum, to preach a holy war against the British devils in Egypt.'

Although this was pretty much what we had judged, as a result of our earlier talks, must be the case, put in those bald terms I confess it sounded a little ridiculous to me at first. But then I recollected that since the time of the Mahdi, who had claimed exactly that same sort of divine inspiration, the people of the Sudan had been living in a kind of ferment of superstitious dread, awaiting further portents. They were thus easy prey to the sort of nonsense which Igorov had invented.

Moreover, it is one thing to laugh at this from the comfort of an armchair in the club, but quite another when you stood there in the Emir's palace, and remembered that Gordon's death, real enough, tragic enough and horrible enough, was the result of exactly this sort of religious fanaticism, and was – at the time of which I write – only ten years in the past.

'I gave him them an escort to Khartoum,' the Emir was saying. 'What was I to believe? And now you say he is a foreigner, an infidel, and a traitor?'

'And a spy,' added Selim cheerfully, for good measure.

'What was I to believe?' the Emir asked again. He slapped his hands on his knees, like a man who comes to a sudden decision, and stood up. 'Well, then,' said he, and

I recognized the tone well enough – it was that of the career diplomat, the man who realizes that one of his decisions has gone wrong, and that the consequence of the blunder seems likely to be the end of his career, or, in the Emir's case, of his life. 'Well, then. We must go to Khartoum and stop him.'

'I had hoped you would say that,' said Sigerson calmly. 'If we get there quickly enough, much may still be saved.'

The Emir turned to a servant who stood nearby. 'Horses!' he called out. 'And quickly, if you would keep your head on your shoulders!'

16

Khartoum

As we rode through the arid lands that stretch between Suakin and Khartoum, the old Emir kept looking back at us over his shoulder, and asking what he could possibly have been expected to do about Igorov. The pace he set was such a breakneck one that we had little opportunity to answer him, even if any of us had thought of an answer to give him.

When we halted for the night in a little hamlet, the Emir lost no time in elaborating on his troubles, present and prospective. 'I shall be called to account for allowing him to get as far as Khartoum,' he assured us, with a morose shake of his head. 'Why, I even gave him some of my personal bodyguard, to speed him on his way!'

'That may not be a bad thing, though,' remarked Sigerson. 'If I may be permitted to offer a suggestion?'

The Emir nodded, and Sigerson began to expound his plan. As he listened, the Emir's face lost some of its woeful look, and by the time Sigerson had done, the Emir not only beamed cheerfully at us, but stood up and actually embraced the mortified Sigerson.

'Your brothers, though uncommunicative, are evidently cunning schemers,' the Emir told Selim, who had, for obvious reasons, done most of the talking on our behalf up until then.

'I have done my humble best to instruct them,' said Selim modestly. 'As to their being close-mouthed, the truth of the matter is that they have worked with the accursed British in Egypt for so long, and been forced to sully their mouths with the ridiculous language – like the braying of a donkey, is it not? – that they have all but lost their Arabic.'

'Indeed?' The Emir looked at us pretty closely at this information, and I inwardly cursed Selim for his stupidity. 'Working with the British, say you?'

'Ah,' said Selim, 'that is their cunning. They pretend to work with the infidel dogs, while secretly doing all they can to undermine their rule. I could tell you tales of espionage, sabotage and all-round treachery that would do your heart good to hear.'

The Emir's face cleared. 'I see. Just the sort of men I get on best with! And the sainted Khalifa, too, will be pleased to meet you.'

I do not know what the others felt about the prospect, but I found my skin crawling at the very thought of meeting the bloodthirsty villain who oppressed the Sudan. However, it would have been fatal to have said anything of the kind, so I tried to look as pleased as I could.

After three or four days through wild, almost empty country, we arrived at Khartoum, an unimpressive collection of low mud huts scattered along one bank of the Nile. The only good thing about the place, it struck me, was that the wind from the desert could blow unimpeded through the streets, and hence carry off to some extent the many and varied stenches that, despite the best efforts of the wind, assailed the nostrils.

'Now,' said the Emir, looking around the place with a keen interest, 'I have been here before, but it was ten years or so ago, and I am not entirely sure of the way.'

I shuddered at the thought of what this cynical old man

might have seen and done on his last visit here. But then, by his own lights, I suppose he was no worse than the rest of them in that God-forsaken place, and his courtly manner had done much to make us forget that he was the representative of the Khalifa, and, I suppose, of the Mahdi before that.

Khartoum struck me as being an eerie place. It had a look of neglect, of being haunted by the ghosts of ancient infamies and all but forgotten tragedies. The fact that the seat of government had been moved to Omdurman, across the Nile, may perhaps have contributed to the feeling that the place had been deserted. Or again, it may well have been that the city was livelier than it appeared to me, that it was the memory of Gordon's death that weighed upon my mind and cast a gloom over the whole place.

Be all that as it may, the old Emir looked about him until he recollected some landmark, then set off, the rest of us following. We halted before a large building, somewhat more imposing, though no cleaner, than its fellows, and the Emir dismounted.

A short, rotund man came scurrying out to greet us, and he and the Emir embraced with many expressions of mutual affection. This man was evidently some local dignitary, he was probably another emir, I imagine, the title is quite common in those parts, but he filled more or less the office of mayor for the city of Khartoum, so I shall call him the mayor to distinguish him from our old friend the Emir of Suakin.

There were introductions all round, and the mayor invited us inside cordially enough, and called for refreshments.

As anyone who has travelled much in those parts will be aware, the process of welcoming guests can be a protracted one, and the mayor was evidently intending all the courteousness that the occasion demanded. The Emir, however, was still apprehensive that we might have arrived too late, and when once the mayor had bid us welcome, the Emir remarked, 'Forgive my boldness, my friend, but we are here on most urgent business. Have two travellers arrived here in the last day or so, a big man with fair skin and a black beard, accompanied by one of our own Dervishes?'

'Indeed,' the mayor nodded. 'They have been here two days, and the city is talking of nothing else.'

'And how so?'

'It is said that they preach a holy war against the British. The Dervish has, naturally, talked to his fellows, and the word has gone to the Khalifa. It is rumoured that he plans to come here, tomorrow or the day after, to see for himself.'

'Does he?' said the Emir. 'Now, my friend, this is all very interesting, for we have followed these two men here from Suakin. They are spies and traitors, and since I sent them here, their continued existence is a danger to me.'

'Oh?' It did not sound as if regard for his old comrade's well-being had a high place in the mayor's catalogue of imperative concerns.

'And to you, of course, since you are responsible for the safety of Khartoum.'

'Oh. Well, I was, naturally, about to say that we must do something about these villains.'

'Softly, old friend, softly. Our brother here has a plan, though we did not know that the saintly Khalifa would be coming here – that is so much the better, now that I think about it. We shall wait until he arrives, meet him before he can see the traitors, and tell him the truth about them. We shall say – and it is true enough, up to a point – that we knew them for what they are, but waited so that the Khalifa himself might deal with them.'

The mayor wriggled in his chair. 'Wonderful, wonderful! Think you that he will deal with them here, or take them to Omdurman?'

The Emir shrugged. 'As to that, it matters little to me. Age has dimmed my pleasure in watching elaborate executions.'

'Oh? Fortunately I have not been so affected.' And the two old rogues roared with laughter, with the rest of us trying to join in as heartily as we decently could.

By this time it was late afternoon, and the mayor said that we should dine with him, and offered us a couple of rooms, a grand one for the Emir, and one not so grand for the rest of the party.

When we had been shown to our room, that we might prepare for the meal later on, I took the opportunity to speak to Sigerson about something that had been bothering me for some time. 'Is it right?' I asked him, 'to denounce even Igorov to these wretches? I have heard some talk of the cruelty of this Khalifa, and I think that, no matter what harm Igorov may have wished to do to Britain, he does not deserve the sort of fate which certainly awaits him at the hands of these butchers.'

Sigerson had the grace to look shamefaced. 'I confess that it is something which has bothered me, too,' he said. 'To kill an enemy in the heat of battle is one thing, but this is something else. The real difficulty is that our own position here is none too secure. Were we in England or France, we should have recourse to the authorities. In Tibet, we were to some extent engaged in open warfare, with no quarter sought or given. Here, we must use all our skill and art merely to avoid a hideous death ourselves at the hands of the Khalifa's torturers. But I am by no means happy about what we proposed. In the desert, it seemed a sensible way of putting a stop to Igorov's schemes, but now –' and he shrugged, and looked most unhappy.

'But then why go through with it?' asked Selim. 'I know that "Byzantine" has become identified with a Machiavellian intricacy, but it seems to me that in this instance the answer is very simple. Why do we not see Igorov ourselves, and tell him that we know everything? That we have given him away to the Khalifa, and that he would be well advised to flee for his life?'

Sigerson's face cleared. 'Excellent!'

Over dinner that evening, we asked the mayor if he knew where Igorov might be found.

'He sits in the ruins of the old palace,' he answered, looking round uneasily.

'What,' said our Emir, 'the place of the devil, Gordon?'

'Aye. It is a strange place,' the mayor explained to us, 'haunted by djinns and other evil spirits.' He shuddered. 'As you will imagine, that has added to the mystery surrounding these men.'

'And this palace is – where, exactly?' asked Selim.

'On the river bank, in such a direction,' the mayor told him, pointing.

We had intended to ask to be excused, pleading fatigue after the ride, but the Emir saved us the trouble, saying precisely what we had planned to say. He was a very old man, so it was understandable, and it saved us from drawing attention to ourselves.

The mayor's house had only an aged watchman by way of a guard, and we easily eluded him, and made our way through deserted alleys and lanes until we reached the river. Gordon's palace was not too hard to find, for the local people had evidently the same distaste for the place as their mayor had displayed, so that there were few new houses round about it.

Even to a man who does not believe in djinns, the palace had a menacing air. It had been burned to the ground at the same time that Gordon had been slain, and only the stumps of the walls remained. Some night bird hooted as we neared the place, and I was sure that, had I been a superstitious

Dervish, I should have taken it for Gordon himself, come to visit the scene of his murder.

We dared not light a lantern or anything of the sort, but there was a rind of a moon low in the sky, and by its sickly beams we picked our way through a forest of blackened and crumbling timbers, and over piles of rubble.

I was in the lead, and after a moment I spied a kind of makeshift tent or shelter in an angle of the wreckage, and changed direction towards it, coming to an abrupt halt as I all but stumbled over what seemed to be a body lying in the debris. I raised a hand to warn the others, and we bent down to see who or what it might be.

It was a man, not Igorov, but an Arab, with a great mop of frizzy hair. And he was not dead, but asleep, snoring loudly.

'Evidently the Dervish,' whispered Sigerson in my ear. 'And Igorov, I take it, is in the tent yonder. What is the Russian for "Prince", I wonder?'

I scratched my head. 'Gospodin?' I hazarded.

'It will have to do. It is at times like this that a man understands the parable of the Tower of Babel.' And he bent down to the flap of the rough shelter, and called out softly.

The tent shook as the sleeper inside woke and sat up, then the flap was thrust aside and Igorov stared out at us. He recognized us almost at a glance, and gave us a broad smile. 'Well, sirs, I take it I need not ask the reason for this call.' He held the flap to one side. 'If you can tolerate a somewhat intimate ambience, please come inside, and I shall light the lamp. The neighbours make no complaint over my eccentricities, thank the Lord.'

We did as he asked, with some difficulty, for the tent was not by any means generously proportioned, and Igorov struck a match and found a stub of candle.

'As you say,' began Sigerson without preamble, 'there is no need to enquire as to why we are here. We have come to warn you that the authorities know who you are, and wait only for the arrival of their master to take the requisite action.'

Igorov rubbed his bushy beard. 'It might seem that such a denunciation could rebound upon the denouncer,' said he. 'After all, your own position here is – an irregular one, shall we say?'

'Can you recite the Holy Koran?' asked Selim.

Igorov looked puzzled.

'I can,' added Selim. 'Or much of it, at any rate. Moreover, we have excellent references, in the shape of two of the local chieftains.'

'H'mm. Then there remains the possibility of an immediate settlement of the matter between us.' And Igorov produced a large army revolver.

'There is really no necessity for that,' Sigerson told him. 'We are all heavily armed –' I may remind you that such was not the case, but Igorov could not know that – 'and in addition to that we have our allies surrounding this place.'

'A sensible precaution,' said Igorov, putting the revolver away. 'So then it must be a hasty au revoir?'

'Think you we shall meet again?' Sigerson asked.

'Oh, I shall make it my business to see that we do,' said Igorov with another broad grin. 'Let me see, Selim Effendi I know well enough, Herr – Sigerson, was it not? I do not think we have met save the once, though I feel I should know you. Were you ever in Russia, perchance?'

'I had the pleasure of visiting Odessa once. In connection with the Trepoff case, which may be familiar to you.'

'Ah.' I could see recognition in Igorov's eyes. 'I should have known. I had not the honour of meeting you then, but there was much talk of the affair, and of your part in it. Your government chose well, Mr – Sigerson. And this young man, yes – the Turkish Embassy, but I fear I forget the name.'

'Dyce, sir,' I told him. 'Lieutenant Dyce.'

'A soldier? Good, good. Yes, I feel we shall meet again, Lieutenant.'

'Under happier circumstances, I trust, sir.'

Igorov laughed. 'Let us hope so.' He hesitated. 'I appreciate the fact that you have come to see me, gentlemen, the local folk do have some curious ideas as to what constitutes entertainment. And now, if you will forgive me, I must pack, though it will not take long.'

'Is there aught you would need for the journey?' asked Sigerson.

'Nothing, thank you.'

'Then we shall say good night, and au revoir, if that is indeed appropriate.'

We took our leave, stepped over the still sleeping Dervish, and returned to our quarters, passing the old watchman, who was also sound asleep, as we did so.

I was all for making good our escape at dawn next day, but Sigerson pointed out that it would have looked most suspicious, and the pursuit would undoubtedly be raised at once. Furthermore, by remaining, we should give Igorov a better start on any pursuit.

A messenger arrived at breakfast, to say that the Khalifa would be there late that afternoon, and would be gracious enough to honour the mayor with his company.

There ensued some frantic preparations, for it was unwise to displease the Khalifa, and I was delighted that these preparations involved our being turned out of our room, for I had little taste for sleeping under the same roof as the madman who ruled the Sudan.

The mayor did not exactly turn us out into the street, but

billeted us on one of his near neighbours, a dignified enough old gentleman, who looked frightened to death at the prospect of being associated with three fanatics such as ourselves. Selim had some talk with him, though, and did much to reassure him, after which Sigerson had a long chat about conditions generally, the results of which he intended, he told me later, to transmit to the authorities in London.

Evening came, and with it the Khalifa and his retinue. We were more or less obliged to go along and do him homage, and it was one of the more distasteful tasks that have come my way. He was not an imposing figure, a little below average height, with the mark of Cain writ as clearly upon his brow as any cut-throat I have ever encountered. His evil little eyes darted up and down us in a most insolent fashion – had one of my native servants dared regard me in such a way, I should have thrashed him on the spot, but we could do nothing save fawn upon the wretch, and tell our tale.

Selim did most of the talking, and the Khalifa nodded as he listened, smirking offensively at the worst tales of treachery and shabbiness.

I was pleased when the hour for dinner arrived, and we, not being invited to the high table, so to speak, could make good our escape, after promising to be on hand early next day to witness the encounter between Igorov and the Khalifa.

We talked to some of the Khalifa's bodyguard, and gained some information as to the disposition, strength and morale of the Sudanese forces, of which information Sigerson again took careful note.

Next day, we marched at the head of the great procession to the old palace. I noticed that many of the common people hesitated about going too near, but the Khalifa, secure with his guards about him, marched into the ruins, and up to the rough shelter.

His disappointment at finding Igorov gone was evident, and had it not been for the fact that the Russian's companion was clearly afflicted of Allah, I do not think his life would have been worth much.

'Word of your magnificence's arrival has reached this rascal,' said the old Emir, 'and he has fled, rather than face your vengeance. A clear proof of his guilt.'

'H'mm.' The Khalifa stared at the Dervish who had travelled with Igorov. 'I suppose you are truly mad, my brother, and not just pretending? I imagine it would be pointless putting you to the torture to discover the whereabouts of your creature?'

The Dervish scratched his head, and smiled foolishly at him.

'H'mm,' said the Khalifa again, the indecision patent in his eyes. Then his brow cleared, and he called out, 'Where is the fellow who came to me with the great news that a saint had arrived in Khartoum, and preached a holy war? Let him be brought forward, that I may reward him properly.'

It transpired, however, that the man concerned had taken no thought for any reward, but gone quietly about his business elsewhere, and the Khalifa cursed him bitterly.

At a break in the flow, Sigerson approached the wretch and said quietly, 'It would be unwise to consider any invasion of Egypt just at the moment, your highness.'

'Indeed? And why so? Stay, let us have some privacy here,' and the Khalifa vented some of his anger by telling his guards to clear the crowds away, which they did in a most ungentle fashion. 'Now, speak.'

'The British are cunning devils,' said Sigerson. 'They would wish you to invade Egypt, for they have vast armies waiting in ambush. Indeed, I am not sure that this spy who has fled your wrath was not an agent of the British, sent here as part of the plot.'

'I see.' The Khalifa's eyes narrowed. 'You are sure of this?'

'Highness,' the Emir put in, 'these men have worked for you against the British in Egypt for many years. They are my own men, true and trusted.'

'Indeed. And so what would you advise?'

'Do nothing,' Sigerson told him. 'Do not attract the attention of the British devils, for they would like nothing better than to have an excuse to avenge Gordon.'

The Khalifa looked around the blackened ruins with some unease. 'I think you are right. I shall return to Omdurman, and linger secure there – for, if aught should befall me, how could my people thrive?'

'Just so,' said Sigerson.

'We did not catch this fellow,' said the Khalifa, 'but you did well to warn me nonetheless. Do you return to Egypt, to continue the good work?'

'If it please you,' Sigerson told him.

'It does, it does. Take some good horses,' he waved a hand magnanimously about him, 'and say that I shall pay any price, if the seller comes to see me in Omdurman. And so, farewell.' And off he went, followed by his entourage.

'What think you to his guards?' Sigerson asked me.

'Not much. They may have taken Gordon by surprise – the garrison here was not a large one – but I cannot think they would last long against a determined force.'

'So I think. If this wretch does not cause any trouble for a time, I think it will be easy enough to re-take the Sudan, and avenge Gordon. I shall inform London to that effect.'

I may add that I believe that 'Sigerson' did just that, and that the invasion and conquest of the Sudan a few years later was the direct consequence of his report.

We now took our leave of the old Emir, and he gave us guides and an escort to the border with Egypt. Incidentally, I heard from Selim later that the Emir decamped at the first hint of the British invasion, and might be seen in Mecca, showing the more gullible pilgrims some of the sights in return for a few coppers. I cannot honestly say that I was sorry at the news, doubtless the old rogue richly deserved hanging twice over, but he was likeable enough.

At the border, we parted with our escort, and rode on alone until we encountered a patrol of British cavalry. To say that they were surprised to encounter us there at that time, and that for a while they treated our story with some caution, is to understate the matter. But I gave them my best parade ground manner, and we eventually convinced them.

A week later, we were in Cairo, and there my story must end.

Part Three

From the journals of Dr John H Watson

17

A postscript

'**D**yce's account ended rather abruptly,' I said.

Holmes took his gaze from the ceiling, and stared at me. 'It was something of an abrupt end to an interesting series of adventures,' he said. 'Dyce returned to his regiment, Selim to his embassy, and I to my old friends in London. My work was done, after all.'

'And the stay in France?' I asked.

'Oh, that was real enough. I travelled from Alexandria to Marseilles, fully intending to make my way to one of the Channel ports, and start looking at the news from England, to see when best to make my entrance. But I met a man with whom I had some acquaintance, and he told me that the director of the new chemical laboratory needed someone to conduct some research into the coal-tar derivatives. I was in no particular hurry, and I have always found the atmosphere of France soothing, so I stayed.'

'And returned when the work there was done?'

Holmes laughed. 'I bumped into Le Villard — you may have some recollection of him? He was there on some case, and we got talking, as you may suppose. It was he who informed me that Sylvius was no longer in London, that he had in fact been observed making a villainous progress through France, on his way to Algeria.'

'Ah, to shoot lions, no doubt?'

'No doubt. Sylvius, you will not need reminding, was one of my most dangerous enemies at that time. He and Moran had stood their trial, but because of my being out of London – or perhaps for a more sinister reason – they had walked free, and whilst they were together in London, they presented an undoubted danger to me. Now only Moran remained, so I decided to return to England without delay. I made my way to Calais, stopping only to have a wax bust made – I had already worked out my scheme to trap Moran, you see. I confess that I was a little apprehensive lest the Customs authorities examine my baggage.'

'How so?' I asked.

'Well, if they found I had a wax bust of myself, it would increase that entirely unjustified reputation for egocentricity which, thanks to your rather sensational accounts, I have laboured under for many years.'

'I suppose so. Did they examine your bags?' I asked with a sudden access of hope.

'No, I am pleased to say. Anyway, I was actually in Calais when news of Adair's death reached me. I knew at once that Moran was the murderer, and took the first boat. The rest you know.'

'Yes.' I looked around the old place. 'This really is like old times, Holmes. I take it that you are now involved in some work on behalf of the government? And that young Wiggins – Mr Wiggins, that is to say – is working with you?'

Holmes nodded. 'He is a good fellow, if a little lacking in imagination.' He stretched luxuriously, and sighed. 'Still, he is only young, by comparison, as you say. And those eight children! My dear fellow, would you believe he has photographs of each of them, and insists on showing them to me at every opportunity?' He shuddered, then looked at me with those piercing eyes of his. 'And you, I take it, are doing some useful and congenial work of your own?'

'Me? Oh – well, you know, Holmes, duty and all that. Stern taskmaster, and all the rest. One has to do what one can, and so forth.' And I echoed his sigh.

'I suppose so. Yes, Wiggins is a good fellow, but there are times when one could wish for someone of one's own age to talk to, someone possessed of one's own Bohemianism of disposition, someone who knows one's mental processes as well as oneself –'

'Holmes!'

'Well?'

'A thought has just occurred to me!'

'Indeed?'

'Indeed, Holmes. And if you would be so kind as to touch the bell, I shall expound it to you over a little supper.'

Author's footnote

There is a relatively small, but highly dedicated, band of enthusiasts which persists in regarding Mr Sherlock Holmes and Dr John H Watson as real men. Members of this band delight in controversy, in formulating their own theories and picking holes in those of other enthusiasts. For these people, one of the most puzzling conundrums in the Holmesian canon – which is full of puzzling conundrums – is the mysterious absence of Holmes from England between 1891, when he was popularly supposed to have died at Reichenbach, and 1894, when he reappeared in the case of 'The Empty House'. Just before Holmes 'died' in 1891, Dr Watson remarked that 'There was something very strange in all this' – and how right he was!

To begin with, we must recall that Holmes had just concluded his investigations into the Moriarty gang, investigations which would result in a massive police action against the gang in a couple of days. Why on earth should Holmes choose to leave England at that crucial juncture? The only explanation I personally can think of is the one suggested in 'The Final Problem' and repeated here, namely that Holmes knew that he must stay alive to testify, or the whole massive police operation might well be thrown away; but even that is far from satisfactory.

Then again, why should Holmes simply disappear from view for almost four years? Particularly when his absence seems to have caused the failure of the case against Colonel

Moran, and perhaps other highly-placed members of Moriarty's gang. Several explanations have been advanced, for instance that Holmes suffered some sort of nervous breakdown, or that after defeating Moriarty he was engaged on a diplomatic mission on behalf of his brother Mycroft. And again, although all these have some appeal, none is entirely convincing.

It would surely have had to be something major which kept Holmes away from England for so long, something unusual which took him to Tibet, Persia, etc.? I do not know if the theory that Moriarty survived at Reichenbach is particularly original – and it almost certainly is not – but I had not thought of it; it was suggested to me by Ian Wilkes, who read an earlier version of this tale, and to whom I extend my thanks.

Thanks are also due to David Stuart Davies, for his help and encouragement; and of course to Martin Breese who has so kindly published the book!

It will perhaps be obvious that I am among the band of enthusiasts; those who share that enthusiasm – or who wish to do so – and who desire to study this problem in more depth should first read (or re-read) the two Conan Doyle stories 'The Final Problem' and 'The Empty House'.

For discussion of various aspects of the problem, try the following:

Martin Dakin, *A Sherlock Holmes Commentary* (Newton Abbot: David and Charles, 1972), pp. 154–161.

John Hall, 'An Account of the Whole Situation', *The Musgrave Papers*, Vol. 7 (Huddersfield: The Northern Musgraves, 1994), pp. 22–36.

Tony Medawar, 'The Final Solution', *The Sherlock Holmes Journal*, Vol. 20, No. 4 (London: The Sherlock Holmes Society of London, Summer, 1992), pp. 118–121.